Experience the Ma ... g
Your Own Ritual Tools

The Crafting and Use of Ritual Tools is your hands-on guide to making and working with a variety of sacred implements. Discover how to design, manufacture, and consecrate your own ritual staff, rune set, wand, ritual knife, and magical shield. Learn about the magical properties of different wood types. Feel the living energy of the wood and bond it with your own essence by the very act of hand-crafting each tool.

Explore an ancient and fulfilling method of religious self-expression by fashioning your own ritual tools by hand. Incorporate symbolism drawn from several different religious and magical systems into the design of your sacred implements and magical practice. Meditate upon your personal staff and uncover the mysteries of working with sacred objects. Consecrate, bless, and charge your magical shield and other implements through rituals that you adapt to suit your spiritual path. Create sacred space, draw down the moon, and perform other acts of magic and worship with the assistance of your personally crafted magical wand or ritual knife. Carve your own rune set for divination and magic. Here is everything you need to get started building a wide array of tools to enhance your magical abilities and further your spiritual development.

Master basic woodworking techniques that will enable you to refinish furniture, make simple home repairs, and further enrich your lifestyle through the merging of your spirituality with the physical act of creating works of art that will serve you for a lifetime—and maybe many other lifetimes as well.

About the Author

Eleanor Harris is a philosopher and owns a successful woodworking company, Archaic Craft, which fashions many personalized religious and magical implements discussed within this book. She is currently writing two books to educate the public about modern pagan religions.

Philip Harris is a half-blood Native American and practices Native American spirituality coupled with the teaching of Christ. Philip has a diploma from a highly credited trade school where he majored in carpentry and woodworking.

Eleanor and Philip Harris reside in Orange County, New York. They invite readers that have questions or experience difficulty with their woodworking projects to write in care of the address below and supply a SASE; every inquiry is welcome and will receive a response.

To Write the Authors

If you wish to contact the author or would like more information about this book, please write to the authors in care of Llewellyn Worldwide and we will forward your request. Both the authors and the publisher appreciate hearing from you and learning of your enjoyment of this book and how it has helped you. Llewellyn Worldwide cannot guarantee that every letter written to the author can be answered, but all will be forwarded. Please write to:

Eleanor & Philip Harris
% Llewellyn Worldwide
PO Box 64383, Dept. K346-8
St. Paul, MN 55164-0383
U.S.A.

The Crafting & Use of Ritual Tools

Step by Step Instructions
to Woodcrafting Religious
& Magical Implements

Eleanor and Philip Harris

Cover design: Lynne Menturweck
Cover photo: Steven Douglas Smith
Interior art: Sandra Tabatha Cicero
Editing: Chic Cicero, Sandra Tabatha Cicero
Book editing: Darwin Holmstrom, Laura Gudbaur, Amy Rost,
    Astrid Sandell
Book design: Astrid Sandell

Library of Congress Cataloging-in-Publication Data
Harris, E. Lynn
     The crafting & use of ritual tools : step-by-step
instructions for woodcrafting religious & magical elements /
Eleanor and Philip Harris. -- 1st ed.
         p.   cm.
     Includes bibliographical references (p.).
     ISBN 1-56718-346-8 (pbk.)
     1. Magic. 2. Ritual. 3. Religious articles. 4. Woodwork.
I. Harris, Philip, 1968-   . II. Title.
BF1623.R66H37   1996
143.4'4--dc20   96-9050
                                                          CIP

Llewellyn Publications
A Division of Llewellyn Worldwide, Ltd.
P.O. Box 64383, St. Paul, MN 55164-0383

Also by Eleanor Harris

Pet Loss: A Spiritual Guide (Llewellyn Publications, 1997)
Ancient Egyptian Divination and Magic (Samuel Weiser, Inc., 1997)

Forthcoming

Escape in Egypt (Third World Press)

Dedication

This book is dedicated to the Ink Mountain Coven for releasing details of their coven workings for this text, the Tree Spirits who made this writing possible, and to our parents—especially Eleanor's father, Charles Ray Lillie, who teaches the fine art of "over-engineering" projects.

Acknowledgements

We would like to thank Chic and Tabatha Cicero for editing this text and providing illustrations. Your excellent work helped make this book possible.

Table of Contents

List of Rituals xiii

Preface xv

Introduction 1

1 Identifying Types of Wood 5

2 The Tools of Woodcrafting 21
Recommended Tools 22
Safety 27
A Magical Work Space 28

3 Ritual Staff Construction and Use 29
A Basic Ritual Staff 30
The Shaman Rattle Staff 43
Sword Staff 48
Making a Sword Handle or "Grip" 52
Ritual Staff Use 55

4   Wand Construction and Use   71

The Basic Ritual Wand   74

Magician's Wand   76

Using the Wand in Ritual   82

5   Ritual Knife Construction and Use   87

The Basic Ritual Knife   90

Ritual Knife Use   99

6   Rune Set Construction and Use   103

Rune Set Construction   105

Rune Divination   109

The Elder Futhark Runes   112

Casting the Runes   121

Two Sample Rune Layouts   122

**7   Medicine and Magical Shield
Construction and Use**   127

Shield Construction   128

Decorating Your Shield   131

Shield Uses   133

8   Carving, Painting, and Wood Branding   137

Carving   137

Painting   143

Paint Markers   145

Ink Markers   145

Wood Branding   145

9   Wood Fillers, Stain, Finish, and Enamel   149

Wood Fillers   150

Stain   153

Finish   157

Paints and Enamels   158

10 Ritual Tool Decoration   161

Useful Materials for Decoration   162

A "Hand-grip" for the Ritual Staff   169

Adding a Crystal to your Wand or Staff   171

Symbols   174

Simple Symbols   176

Intermediate Symbols   178

Complex Symbols   181

Examples of Ritual Tool Decoration   183

Selected Symbolism for Ritual Tools   186

Choosing Your Symbols   189

A Ritual to Enhance Your Artistic Abilities   190

11 Ritual Tool Meditation and Consecration   195

Bonding with Your Tool   196

Meditation   196

Visualization   197

Bonding Meditation Exercise   198

The Pathway of Trees Meditation   202

Consecration of Your Ritual Tools   207

Consecration Ritual   207

Resources Guide   213

Suggested Reading   215

Rituals

Circle Casting   55

Calling the Elements   57

Invoking Deity   59

Drawing Down the Moon (Staff)   60

Ritual Invocation   61

Imbolc Ritual   62

Raising the Cone of Power   64

Grounding   67

Drawing Down the Moon (Wand)   82

Handfasting   83

Evocation   85

Consecration of the Cakes and Ale   100

A Healing Spell   133

A Ritual to Enhance Your Artistic Abilities   190

Consecration Ritual   207

Preface

Many people prefer to hand-craft their own ritual tools instead of purchasing more expensive, clone-manufactured, commercial versions. As practicing pagans, we understand the desire to use self-created, personalized religious tools that reflect our sacred spirituality and symbolism.

This text provides instruction for the construction of various ritual tools commonly used in contemporary pagan religious and magical practices. From raw, natural wood, you can hand-craft ritual tools of equal or better quality than those commercially available. Using personalized tools within your religious and magical realm reflects your unique religious beliefs, magical practices, and personal symbolism.

Why choose wood for constructing your ritual tools? We believe that wood is a sacred sub-element that consists of a life force not found in the metals and glass used in commercially made ritual tools. Wood is an instrument of the life force energies of our Creator. It is a living part of nature. When you construct a wooden tool to use in ritual, the wood will not rot. Its life force will remain alive to assist you in all your spiritual and magical ventures.

In this book we've presented the techniques for constructing a ritual staff, wand, ritual knife, rune set, and magical shield in a simplified manner, using woodworking techniques easily understood by the beginner. You do not need prior knowledge, expertise, or carpentry skills to follow these instructions.

You can master basic woodworking techniques that will benefit you beyond the crafting of ritual tools; the information within this text can be used as an excellent reference guide for the novice or experienced woodworker in basic furniture refinishing, furniture or craft repair, and arts and crafts.

We will guide you step-by-step through the designing, crafting, decorating, and use of your ritual tools. We will:

- Explore how to identify wood types at the lumber yard and in nature.

- Learn the magical properties of different wood types.

- Show you the different woodworking tools commonly found around the house.

- Provide simple, clear instructions for creating your own ritual staff, wand, knife, rune set, and magical shield.

- Instruct you on how to incorporate these tools into your own religious and magical practices.

- Teach you basic wood carving, branding, and painting techniques, and how to apply wood fillers, stain, finish, and enamels.

- Explore inexpensive and traditional decorations.

- Examine the symbolism found in several different religious and magical systems.

- Provide you with appropriate meditation and consecration exercises so you may begin to bond with and use your tools.

It is our hope that the information within this text will stimulate your creativity and enable you to enjoy the challenge of crafting your own ritual tools. In fashioning your own ritual tools by hand, you are combining your energies with those of the wood, and your creativity will provide your tool with a uniqueness that sets it apart from any other. This can only strengthen any duty the tool is used for in your practice. It is an extension of you that will provide religious and magical service for years to come!

Introduction

It is certainly not a new concept to fashion religious and magical tools from wood. Our ancestors recognized the strength and durability of wood. They regarded it as a sacred gift of nature, symbolic of deity and strength within battles. Wood was held in high regard as the raw material of choice for the tools of the wise, the noble, and the sorcerer and sorceress.

Examples of symbolic wooden tools can be found throughout the history of mankind. Vikings practiced combat on the shores of new lands with wooden staffs; young Viking boys played with sticks and mimicked their fathers, hoping to one day be great warriors and be granted a staff of their own. Egyptian Gods are depicted in hieroglyphics holding the wooden Uas, a staff with the top carved as the head and ears of an animal and the bottom forked. The Uas was a symbol of authority and divinity. The High Priest of the ancient Jewish San Hedron carried a crook (a shepherd's staff) to display his religious authority. The mighty Celts carried a staff called a stang, forked at the top and pointed at the bottom. Jesus Christ advised each of his disciples to take only their staffs as they separated across lands to spread his teachings.

Ritual staffs were not the only important archaic tool made of wood. The earliest knives for combat and religious and magical practice had wooden handles and blades of flint or beaten stone; sometimes they even had blades made of wood. The Scotch carried Scottish dirks, beautiful knives crafted of maple wood. Later, in the mid-1770s, the dirk's wooden handle was replaced with black ebony.

Through study we find that in all historical periods the world over, most ancient knives, daggers, and weaponry were crafted with wooden handles. This was not simply because there was plenty of wood available—in all civilizations wood was held sacred to some degree, particularly in Egypt, where gold was common and trees were not. Native Americans gathered sacred wood to make tomahawks, war axes, peace pipes, drumming sticks, flutes, and medicine shields.

In North America the branches of the willow tree may have been typical for this use. Modern pagan religions, such as Wicca, certainly favor the willow's long, flexible branches for crafting wands. Contemporary shamans prefer using willow branches for crafting medicine shields.

In ancient times rune sets were typically made of wood, bone, or stone. Historically, the Elder Futhark runes were handmade exclusively from wood.

Ancient people, lacking the burdens of our sophistication and knowledge of modern psychology, found and worshipped the deific presence in the lofty denizens of the forests of their world.[1]

Those of us who grew up in one of the Christian sects may remember frequent reference in the Bible to the Cedars of Lebanon.[2] This tree was held in high regard, considered holy, and worshipped. It was, in essence, the high holy tree of the culture that spawned Christianity.[3] In culture after culture, age after age, the human soul has responded to the spirit of the trees, asking questions and receiving answers.[4]

The wattles, or growths that form on the Rowan tree, were thought to hold all knowledge; thus, the wattles were valued and the tree considered oracular.[5] Certain Roman officers known as lictors carried Rowan rods as a symbol of their authority, as did various other officials of the time.[6]

May Day, (Beltane, May 1st), a fertility rite, was celebrated throughout Europe and Britain into the 1700s, despite its being prohibited by one Parliament in 1644. The practice has been revived and continues today, centered around a standing phallic symbol, the Maypole, which was originally a sacred tree specifically cut for the festival purpose.[7]

The Maypole, much like the ritual staff, indicates the timeless reverential use of the sacred trees and their wood for the purposes of magic and the invocation of deities.

Throughout history and in every culture, mankind has used the branches of trees for religious and magical rites. Branches, flowers, or fruit removed from sacred trees continued to carry the holiness and sanctity of the tree within.[8]

Shamanism teaches that a tree spirit, unlike a human spirit, remains in one place. However, if a partnership is formed with a human, the tree spirit can attain a certain mobility and extend the range of its awareness. It does this by giving up a part of itself—a branch perhaps—which retains the spirit of the tree within it. Such a piece is referred to by shamans as "livewood." By fashioning the livewood into a staff, wand, medicine shield, or other object, the shaman gains access to the tree's wisdom and knowledge, and works in partnership with it.[9]

A tree is like a pipeline from the sky to the earth.[10] It is a living pipeline that carries energy. The same life force energy surges through all living things. When you embrace someone you feel good energy surging between the two of you. This is the same life force that is in trees.[11]

This is only a snippet of the vast information available regarding the worship of trees and the use of sacred woods in ancient practices and tools. Extensive coverage of this subject would be a book in itself! (Should you be interested in the historical study of sacred trees and woods, we have provided a list of books in the Suggested Reading section at the end of this text.)

Many of the objects we employ in everyday life are made of wood, yet rarely are we taught of wood's ancient significance and countless uses. As you begin the work of crafting your ritual tools, contemplate this—how is it that wood, if preserved and maintained, never ceases to exist? Maintained wood will continue its life and overcome decay. This is another reason your ritual tools are best made of wood. They will serve you a lifetime—and maybe many other lifetimes as well.

Endnotes

1. Pattalee Glass-Koentop, *Year of The Moon, Season of Trees* (St. Paul: Llewellyn Publications, 1991), 9.
2. Ibid., 9.
3. Ibid.
4. Ibid.
5. Ibid.
6. Ibid.
7. Ibid., 9, 10, 210, 13.
8. Ibid., 12.
9. Kenneth Meadows, *Shamanic Experience: A Practical Guide to Contemporary Shamanism*, (Rockport, MA: Element Inc., 1991), 78.
10. Sun Bear and Wabun, *The Medicine Wheel Earth Astrology* (New York: Prentice Hall Press, 1980), 201.
11. Ibid., 202.

1

Identifying Types
of Wood

This chapter deals with identifying wood—not identifying tree species. Many people who desire "naturally acquired" wood do not realize that there are many varieties of trees in a single tree family. When searching for your wood source in nature, you must rely on a book or guide to aid in recognizing the tree type by its bark and leaves—and depending on where you live, some tree types may not be commonly found. We decided to leave "tree identifying" to the experts, as describing every tree type is beyond the scope of this book. You can refer to the Suggested Reading section for a list of some books that will help you identify tree types in order to obtain the wood you desire directly from nature.

The first decision you need to make as you begin your ritual tool is whether to obtain your wood commercially or naturally. There are conflicting opinions in the contemporary pagan community as to which source is best, and some pagans insist that the magical properties and energies in trees are lost once their wood is commercially produced. After crafting ritual tools from both commercial and naturally acquired wood, we feel there is no significant difference. The commercially obtained wood works just as well in ritual practice as wood taken directly from a tree.

Sometimes wood is difficult to identify and obtain in either case—commercially or naturally. Commercial establishments label the wood in display sections, making this step easier. However, not all wood types are commercially available due to cost or lack of use in the furniture industry. Venturing into nature offers access to some of those woods not commercially available, but identifying the correct tree can be a problem.

During your search, you may come across books or other sources exhibiting photographs of a variety of wood surfaces. Although informative, it is very difficult to distinguish one wood type from another through photographs, whether they are in color or black-and-white. We mention this so that when you take a guidebook with you into nature, you will not become frustrated when attempting to identify the wood type of a chosen tree from the examples in such books. For this reason, we have not included photographs in this book.

To give an example, let's say you have a guidebook that does not assist in identifying trees, but does show the wood identity of each tree. You begin to investigate the woodland in your area and discover that the wood surface beneath the bark of each tree has similar pigment and texture. You refer to the photographs within the guidebook, look at your chosen tree's wood, and become annoyed that suddenly all wood (with a few exceptions, such as cherry) looks alike. We cannot express too strongly the importance of obtaining guidebooks of both tree and wood identities.

One guidebook that assists the seeker in this process is *The Audubon Society Field Guide to North American Trees* by Elbert Luther Little. (Knopf, 1980).[1] Obviously, the book can be useful no matter your geographical area, and the Audubon Society offers books on this subject in two volumes, one for the eastern region of the United States and one for the western region. For individuals interested in learning about trees, it is an excellent source. Easy to read and user-friendly, this text provides color photographs of leaves, tree bark, tree measurements, branch consistency, and every single attribution that differentiates one tree from another. If you cannot locate your chosen tree in your area, the book provides detailed information on tree families that will assist you in obtaining wood from another tree type in the same family. For example, the oak family is extremely diverse—from swamp chestnut oak to chinkapin oak, the list is extensive. The shape and color of a leaf, the coarseness and color of tree bark, the scent of the wood beneath, whether it is a fruit or nut bearing tree, the type of flowers the tree has, and other characteristics, are so well defined within the field guide that you will be able to conduct your search in nature the day you obtain the book.

What many people don't realize is that identifying trees during winter is more difficult than during any other season. Although you may have a guidebook to identify each tree bark, sometimes that is not enough since the physical appearances of various types of tree bark are often similar. Height and branch formation would help in your quest, but these traits are also similar in many trees. When trees have their foliage, all physical attributes are present and will make identification easier.

Let's examine the silver maple. This tree is common in the northeastern part of the United States. In the spring and summer the silver maple exhibits its three-lobed, simple leaves and keys, otherwise referred to as *samaras*—dry one-seeded fruits with a wing (as children, many of us played with these "helicopter propellers"). By examining these attributes and the characteristics of the tree's gray-colored bark, which becomes furrowed into long, scaly, shaggy ridges, one can identify the tree by checking a guidebook for the tree's geographical region, branch formation, diameter of trunk, and height. It would be unwise to assume that every tree with keys is a maple; ash, box elder, elm, and other trees have them as well.

Don't consider the investigation of your desired tree as impossible or too troublesome. The fine-points of tree identification may seem overwhelming at first. Not so. If you had never driven a car before, and were taught by word of mouth, you'd feel as if it was an overwhelming task until you were actually taught within the automobile and learned through the experience of driving. The same applies to finding your desired tree species.

At the end of this chapter is a list with descriptions of various wood types, their availability, a brief history of their use in furniture, magical properties, and information on applying the best finish for each wood type. Obviously, there are hundreds of wood types traditionally used for ritual tools that are easy to obtain. If you are seeking a wood that is not on the list provided here, call your local lumber yard to find out if it is commercially available, or investigate books mentioned in the Suggested Reading section to find out if your wood type can be acquired from trees in your region.

Included within each description is a commercial cost estimation that notes if a wood type is expensive or inexpensive. However, the cost of wood can vary greatly depending on your region of the country. For precise cost, determine the wood type, length, and width needed for your project, and call local lumber yards for prices.

The magical properties given for each tree or wood type are a collection of Shamanic and Celtic descriptions compiled through years of studying the role of various trees in religion and magic. We have found that no matter what your spiritual tradition is with regard to magical practice with trees or their wood, these descriptions are an accurate portrait of each wood's magical significance.

Amber Wolfe's book *In The Shadow of the Shaman: Connecting with Self, Nature and Spirit* (Llewellyn Publications, 1988), addresses the tree's role in Shamanism. This book presents three charts—"Plant World Totems," the "Chart of Trees," and the "Shamanic Self-Healing Chart"—which demonstrate the tree's influence in magical-spiritual practices. The author's "Chart of Trees" explains the connection between certain tree species to each of the four cardinal directions. It also touches on the ritual staff's use in magical-spiritual growth.

Wolfe also provides an example of her experience with the ritual staff. In the section called "Riding the Wheel of the North," she describes how she acquired her beloved ritual staff without actually extracting it from its mother tree. A tornado, a known destructive force of nature, actually served as a constructive force when it caused this particular branch to break from its tree. This phenomena attracted her spiritually. The fallen branch was "reborn" into her Earth-centered spiritual path. She states that her ritual staff provides a balance between her Wiccan and Native American Shamanic practices, once again reinforcing the prominent use of the ritual staff throughout diverse human religions.

When choosing the ideal wood for your ritual staff, knife, wand, or other project, consider its availability, commercial cost, color, and magical property. The magical properties we've listed do not follow pagan law for wooden ritual aids—they are guidelines. Any wood is a gift of nature, holds valuable energies, and can be used for ritual practice. Use your own instincts and choose the wood that is most appealing to you. Your attraction to a certain kind of wood ensures its performance in your ritual.

If you choose to acquire your wood commercially, do not be shy about asking for assistance from lumber yards and other establishments that sell wood. Ask for samples showing wood color and grains (even paint stores have such samples available). If a chosen wood is too expensive, ask the salesperson for other, less expensive types of wood that resemble it, perhaps something from the same tree family. If you can't find exactly what you want, other types of wood can be stained to imitate the preferred wood.

The basic techniques for finding and preparing your wood, whether you select commercial stock or naturally acquired wood, can be found in chapter 3.

No list can contain every wood type available. We have chosen to list those most popular for ritual tools and accessories in contemporary pagan practices. Your religious or magical denomination may recommend one of the wood types listed below in an attempt to comply with an ancestral tradition. As you read the description of each wood type, you might notice certain terminology that you are not familiar with. *Hardwood* indicates a tough, heavy timber that doesn't come from a cone-bearing tree, or evergreen. *Softwood* is wood from a cone-bearing tree that is easily cut and light in weight. Softwoods are best for the beginner who wants a wood that is easy to work with and carve. It is usually less expensive than hardwood and easier to find in nature. The term *virgin* is used to describe a wood without a finish. At times a wood will look its best when its natural pigment is not stained or finished. There is no sense in covering up virgin wood with a stain if its natural color is appealing.

Types of Wood

Apple

Apple wood is difficult to obtain commercially because it is not often used in furniture or home building. Its commercial cost varies. Apple trees are often found in private yards, roadsides, and forest clearings, usually growing in ground with moist soil. Apple wood's magical properties often concern the idea of honor, and it is especially sacred to the Goddess. Apple is also known as the tree of love. Magical spells for love often end by throwing apple wood upon a carefully made fire to symbolically cast the spell.

Shamans have associated the apple tree with making right choices and decisions from challenging options. The apple is protective and helpful in those areas of human activity in which talents and skills need to be nurtured and developed through consistent care and persistent practice. It emphasizes concentration.[2]

Flails made of apple wood were used to thresh grain and are of such ancient design that they were one of the symbols of the pharaohs of Egypt.[3]

Ash

This inexpensive hardwood is easy to obtain at lumber yards. It is a heavy, tough wood often used in furniture manufacturing, particularly for bentwood pieces. This wood is preferred for tool handles and is especially useful for the construction of ritual staffs, wands, ritual knife handles, and an assortment of other projects. Magically, ash is a sacred tree, a medicine tree, and embodies the principal of reverence. Its primary magical properties are sensitivity, intuition, awareness, and peace. The ash provides a key to understanding the holistic nature of the universe and shows how the material and the spiritual are connected. It also shows how one's inner thoughts ultimately find expression in the outer world of physical manifestation. The ash tree helps people change their lifestyles, attain a right relationship with the Earth, and link their outer and inner worlds.[4]

The God, Woden (Wotan, Odin, Gwydion), is said to have used ash as his steed, taking it from the Norns (a form of the Triple Goddess in religion), who dispensed justice beneath its branches. In

Scandinavian mythology the enchanted ash, Ygdrasill, is the cosmic world tree, its roots and branches extending throughout the universe.[5]

In Ireland, three of the Five Magic Trees (Tree of Tortu, Tree of Dathi, and Branching Tree of Usnech) were ash. Their fall in 665 C.E. is said to symbolize the triumph of Christian faiths over paganism.[6]

In contemporary Witchcraft, the staff or stake of a Witch's besom (broom) is still composed of ash. Several different wood types are used in its construction, including birch twigs to entangle and expel evil spirits. The ash stake is used for protection against drowning, and the osier[7] of willow bindings are in honor of Hecate.[8]

The ash is versatile in its uses. It was used to make kings' thrones and for the shafts of weapons and spears. Employed in rain-making ceremonies, the ash is said to court the lightning.[9]

Ash may be best identified by its grayish-white or, at times, brownish color. Its grain patterns are marked, and the wood has open pores. The ideal finish for ash is a clear finish over virgin or stained wood.

Beech

This dense, strong hardwood is not easily obtained commercially, but when found it is usually inexpensive. In furniture manufacturing, it is frequently used for turned and bent work. The magical property of beech is aid in achieving goals and wishes by giving a person organizational skills.

The beech tree is linked with the thirst for knowledge that nourishes the soul. It is the guardian of lost wisdom, a door of access to mystical insight for those who quest for it with love in their hearts. It guards against repeating mistakes and helps in the establishment of a firm foundation for future action.[10]

Beech is best identified by its soft cream color, which is at times pinkish with brown flecks. It is a difficult wood to carve because it is dense. When used, beech looks most attractive with a clear finish over virgin or stained wood.

Birch

Although birch is inexpensive and easy to obtain commercially, it is a very difficult hardwood for the novice to use. It is strong, stiff, and heavy, which makes it a challenge in woodworking—especially for woodcarving. In furniture manufacturing it is often stained and used to imitate more expensive woods such as walnut or cherry. Birch has the key magical property of support. It is very powerful for purification and protection, and is said to give the stern yet gentle maternal care that is from the Goddess.

Birch often represents the Goddess or female principal. In northern European countries, the Goddess of Spring, or the Maiden, is seen as the Birch Goddess. Birch may be added to a Beltane Fire to symbolize the Goddess.[11] The birch is an almost universal symbol of fertility.

Ritual staffs made from birch are wonderful for attuning with the Goddess in her many forms. High Priestesses in covens that use the ritual staff often hand-craft them from birch to help invoke the Goddess during ritual.

In magical workings the silver birch is said to strengthen and clarify the image of what is desired; it brings the intention into sharp focus and guards the image from diffusion. Silver birch indicates new beginnings and an upsurge of energy usually associated with things that are fresh and new.[12]

Cedar

A fairly hard and brittle wood, cedar is neither the easiest nor most preferred wood for woodworking. Inexpensive and easy to obtain commercially, cedar is often used as a raw material in drawers, chests, and any furnishings that have storage purposes. The scent of cedar maintains a pleasant smell in storage spaces and it is known to repel moths. Cedar's red color and aromatic characteristics make it a desirable choice for seekers from many spiritual paths. Its magical property is divination, and cedar's aroma and color aid in meditation and healing, as well as in divination. Since cedar banishes negativity and promotes clear readings, we feel it is best to use cedar as a storage container for all your divination supplies, such as a decorative wooden box to hold tarot cards.

There are few among us who aren't familiar with the rich scent of cedar. The sweet smell of cedar promotes spirituality. Inhale this sweet, antiseptic, calming fragrance before religious rituals to deepen your connection with deity.[13] Its spiritual qualities make the fragrance of cedar ideal for bringing yourself into balance. Smell the aroma and visualize yourself as poised, calm, and in control of your own life.[14]

In the ancient world, cedar from Lebanon was highly prized—so much so that only a small number of trees remain standing in that country.[15] This fragrant tree was also much used by Plains Indians who placed cedar twigs on hot stones in sweat lodges for purification. The Pawnee burned twigs of cedar, much like the morning-glory bush, to banish nightmares and nervous conditions.[16]

Cedar has pronounced knotty patterns that do not take well to carving. In ritual tool decoration, cedar is best left with its natural surface intact.

Cherry

This wood is quite hard and has a tight grain that is resistant to warping. Cherry is easy to obtain and is moderately inexpensive. This wood is used commercially for good-quality furnishings. Its magical property is fruitfulness and cherry promotes fertility, growth, renewal, and warmth in emotion.

The High Priestess of the Ink Mountain Coven, a Gardnerian Wicca coven active in the eastern United States since 1986, enlightened us as to how the word "cherry" came to be associated in modern times to the usually degrading terminology in reference to a young lady's virginity. According to her, this folk term began ages ago when the cherry tree was highly revered for its fertility symbolism. Folklore attributed a woman's genital to the cherry fruit of the tree because both were symbols of fertility and the ability to give birth or fruit. It is only in our modern era that the term has been used in a distasteful manner.

The High Priestess also indicated that the Ink Mountain Coven uses a cherry wood ritual staff during the celebration of Imbolc, Ostara (Spring Equinox), and various other ritual and magical practices concerning the Goddess and fertility.

Identified by its warm red-brown color that becomes richer with age and exposure to the sun, cherry is well-suited for ritual tools that are used outdoors since it resists warping and will not bleach in color. Cherry wood has small pores and does not require filling. (Filling is for large-pored woods to prevent uneven absorption of stains, enamels, and other treatments. This technique is explained in chapter 9). Cherry wood looks best unstained and with a clear finish.

Elm

This wood has a medium hardness, but is suitable for various types of woodworking. Elm is difficult to purchase commercially, although it is used frequently in bentwood chair manufacturing. When found commercially, elm is inexpensive.

American elm, also known as rock elm, is light brown with a straight grain that has light and dark variations. English elm is coarse, pale brown, and has an irregular grain. American elm is the best choice because it is easy to work with and has an attractive grain pattern.

Little is known of religious or magical use of elm wood. The magical property of elm is sometimes disputed in contemporary paganism. We understand elm to promote philosophical thought. Hackleberry wood is of the elm family. It is purported to have graced many ancient rites. The twigs or leaves were used to adorn altars during seasonal rituals. A pagan friend informed us that she has used an elm branch for her ritual wand and has felt that she has gained philosophical insight through its use. There is certainly no reason why elm should not be used for crafting your ritual tools. Who knows? Perhaps you will discover qualities within the elm that will enhance your own spiritual and magical endeavors.

Elm wood can be carved with your personal symbols. If you want a more appealing look to the wood, you can stain the surface and give it a clear finish.

Hickory

A strong, durable wood, hickory is a member of the walnut family. It is often used in cabinet-making due to its physical strength. Though difficult to obtain commercially, hickory is fairly priced when found.

The magical property of hickory is endurance. It is best used by those who are firm in their beliefs and brave in their actions, as hickory aids in difficult magical work where anxiety resides. Other than our personal experience with hickory used for endurance in ritual practice, little is known of its spiritual and magical properties. These definitions are derived from our own use of the wood.

Hickory is identified by its reddish-brown pigment. Often the wood is finished with a clear finish over the natural surface to enhance the color, or given a stain of hickory shade to deepen color tones.

Maple

An extremely hard and strong wood, maple is difficult to obtain commercially and is expensive when found. With a fine, even texture, maple is used for the highest quality furniture. The grain is almost always straight with little pores and appears at times to have a bird's eye or curly pattern. Without a doubt, maple is one of the most beautiful wood types.

Maple's magical property is kinship. Ritual tools made of maple aid in problems or magical work directed to relatives, friends, or lovers. It promotes energy, healing, and enthusiasm in relationships.

Maple wood is identified by its amber, white, or cream-white pigment. The red of maple wood, as seen in furniture, comes from stain applied to the wood surface. Maple looks best when stained red or given a clear finish over the virgin wood.

Oak

Perhaps the most popular hardwood, oak is easy to obtain and is commercially inexpensive. This durable, strong wood has a grain that you can feel with your fingers. It can be given a nice, smooth surface by sanding, if desired. In furniture manufacturing, oak is used for figured veneers and on older furniture in need of repair.

Its key property is magic, which makes oak a popular choice for contemporary pagan practitioners. It promotes higher planes of awareness, aids in shifting of consciousness for magical work, and philosophical thought. Because of its durability, oak is suitable for outdoor ritual, nature magic, and spiritual enlightenment. Many pagans feel there is no better wood than oak for wands, staffs, and other ritual tools.

Oak's special qualities of strength and durability come from the fact that it grows slowly but develops steadily. Oak stresses the importance of patience and the fact that great things develop from small beginnings. It promotes the power of inner achievement and the need not to allow the limitations of logic-based systems of knowledge to smother hopes and aspirations.[17]

Oak symbolizes the God, or male, principle in nature. In Celtic countries, the Druids worshiped in sacred oak groves and used every part of the oak tree for ritual purposes. It is also from the oak that the

Druids gathered the sacred mistletoe, the white berries of which were seen as representing the semen of the Lord of the Forest, linking the oak to the male principal.[18]

In Spring rites, the ritual staff is used for many purposes, such as the Priapic Staff or wand. This tool is an emblem of the God; the primary phallic symbol. In many pagan religions it is traditionally made of oak.

For spiritual and magical rites involving astrology, oak is ruled by Saturn.

Oak's color ranges from pale gray to rose-brown. The wood surface of oak is best left natural. Many pagans believe stain and clear finish clog the natural energies that the sacred oak projects.

Pecan

This tree is a relative of hickory and also belongs to the walnut family. Though difficult to obtain commercially, pecan is inexpensive to purchase. Strong and durable, its hardness is medium and the wood can be easily worked. It is often used for cabinet-making.

Pecan's magical property is good fortune. The richness of its fruit symbolizes luxury, making pecan a wonderful wood for spells regarding finances and good luck. Little is known of further spiritual and magical properties of this wood.

Pecan is identified by its reddish-brown pigment that usually has dark streaks. Pecan wood surfaces are often left natural or stained in natural shades to deepen their color tones.

Pine

This wonderful, inexpensive, readily available wood is easy to obtain commercially. Its softness is perfect for wood-crafting and ideal for the beginner. When carving pine, be careful to carve with the grain, otherwise the wood flakes will cause a jagged appearance. Often, pine is used for unfinished pieces or reproductions in the furniture industry.

Pine's magical property is expression. The stretching branches and evergreen tapering characteristic of the pine promote spiritual growth through emotional expression.

The Ink Mountain Coven suggests that new members craft a ritual staff, wand, or ritual tool of pine to assist them in spiritual and emotional development within the coven.

The pine family includes the fir, which has an extensive history in ancient spiritual and magical rites as well as a place in folklore. Because fir is within the pine family, we did not list it separately within this text.

The fir is the tree of immortality. Sacred to the Goddess of birth and rebirth, the evergreen fir tree is a symbol of the forces of life overcoming the forces of death and decay.[19]

Evergreens bear out the characteristics of birth and rebirth. Both Attis and Osiris, in some myths, were imprisoned in pine trees or logs, and the logs were burned a year later, freeing the two respective Gods through rebirth. The symbolism of the pine cone in religious ceremonies represents resurrection.[20]

Ritual tools made of pine are excellent choices for those in quest of new beginnings and rebirth. Its woodsy scent is ideal for those seeking a form of aromatherapy during ritual.

Pine wood is best preserved with clear finish, particularly if used outdoors. Its wood warps quickly from temperature and climate.

Poplar

This wood is excellent for woodworking. It has a soft, light weight, and an even texture. Poplar is inexpensive and easy to find commercially. It is primarily used for plywood and to imitate other woods in manufacturing furniture.

The magical properties of poplar are protection and resolution. Poplar wood ritual tools used during astral projection, meditation, spiritual communication, or any exercises of the psyche are ideal for protection against negativity and for resolution of problems. Poplar is in the willow family, and they share many qualities.

In Greek mythology, Hercules traveled to the springs of Ister to bring the white poplar back to Olympia. Poplar staffs were used by the Hyperboreans, the servants of Apollo.[21]

Wood from the poplar tree was once made into shields, indicating that the tree not only resists attack but strengthens attempts of resolution in the face of difficulties. The poplar is a symbol of hope and an expression of encouragement in doing what the heart tells you is right. Its leaves whisper in the wind as if each is speaking. The poplar encourages you to whisper your silent thoughts and to express your feelings with gentleness.[22]

Poplar is identified in colors of white, yellowish-brown or, at times, light yellow. The wood may be stained, and takes stain very well—an attribute that is helpful to the beginner. It is often painted with color enamel as well.

Redwood

Good for woodwork, redwood is strong, light, and not very hard. It is not readily available commercially, although it is used to manufacture fine pieces of furniture and outdoor furniture, such as picnic tables. Extremely resistant to rot and weather conditions, it is wonderful for outdoor use. The cost for redwood is not great.

The magical properties of redwood are honesty and truth, but religious and magical use of redwood is not well documented. Since the redwood has needle-like or scale-like leaves, it is considered by some as an evergreen. This may provide an explanation for the lack of further magical-spiritual information on the use of redwood, and its magical uses are similar to those of the pine family.

Since many contemporary pagans enjoy the creation of new traditions as well as ancient ones, this wood is ideal for experimenting with religious and magical practices. You may be the one to reveal undiscovered magical properties within this gorgeous tree.

Redwood is identified by its handsome reddish-brown color. Due to its beauty and workability, it is unnecessary to stain the surface. Because redwood is weather resistant, you do not need to apply a clear finish unless you desire a glossy shine. Because there are only fifteen species of redwood in North America, it may be difficult to find in your area. A commercial source would be your best bet for acquiring this wood.

Willow

The wood of willow is not easy to obtain commercially, but the willow family includes poplar, which is commercially available. If you are unable to extract a branch from a willow tree in your area, acquiring poplar from a commercial source is your best alternative. Willow wood is not common in commercial woodwork, except in the case of wicker furniture.

Not all willow trees have "weeping" branches. The most popular willow has branches that are long, flexible, and gentle.

The magical property of willow is healing. Fevers and headaches are said to be healed by the willow.[23] Willow was the herbal medicine containing the pain-relieving effects of aspirin, and it is still widely used today. If you are involved in healing magic, then the use of a ritual tool made of willow, such as a wand or medicine shield, can benefit your practice.

Willow is known as the tree of death in some archaic references. It is sacred to the Greek Goddess Hecate, and its association with both the dark half of the Wheel of the Year and the dark phase of the moon link it to Witchcraft.[24] Words such as witch, wicker, and wicked are all said to have derived from the willow tree.[25]

In some pagan religions willow is associated with the moon, and its wood serves as a primary wand or ritual staff during all rites concerning moon cycles and magic work on certain moon phases. The willow's pliable branches were used for basket weaving and for stockades and thatch supports.

Willow symbolizes the importance of being receptive and nurturing, drawing things together in proper balance, and the need for protection and support. Willow teaches the need for adaptability and, in a world of changing values, of finding satisfaction in the process rather than the ultimate goal.[26]

It would be best to seek willow wood directly from a tree rather than commercially. Willow trees can be found in almost all geographic areas of the United States and are often found around bodies of water, golf courses, and public parks.

It is not necessary to stain or finish willow wood. The gentle beauty and grace it embodies is best enjoyed in its natural state.

Many wood types not listed here are also available to you. We have attempted to list those wood types most sought after for their historical use in pagan rites, magical properties, purchase cost, and availability, both commercially and in nature.

Endnotes

1. ISBN: 0394507606 for the eastern region of the U.S., ISBN: 0394507614 for the western region.
2. Kenneth Meadows, *Shamanic Experience: A Practical Guide to Contemporary Shamanism* (Rockport, MA: Element Inc., 1991), 134.
3. Pauline Campanelli, *Wheel of The Year: Living The Magical Life* (St. Paul: Llewellyn Publications, 1992), 47.
4. Meadows, *Shamanic Experience*, page 134.
5. Pattalee Glass-Koentop, *Year of the Moon, Season of Trees: Mysteries & Rites of Celtic Tree Magic* (St. Paul: Llewellyn Publications, 1990), 210.
6. Ibid.
7. A long rod-like twig used in basketry.
8. Glass-Koentop, *Year of the Moon*, 210.
9. Ibid., 211.
10. Meadows, *Shamanic Experience*, 134.
11. Campanelli, *Wheel of the Year*, 46.
12. Meadows, *Shamanic Experience*, 135.
13. Ibid., 18.
14. Ibid., 71.
15. Cunningham, Scott, *Magical Aromatherapy* (St. Paul: Llewellyn Publications, 1992), 18.
16. Ibid., 72.
17. Meadows, *Shamanic Experience*, 135.
18. Campanelli, *Wheel of the Year*, 46-47.
19. Ibid., 48.
20. Glass-Koentop, *Year of the Moon*, 200.
21. Ibid., 203.
22. Meadows, *Shamanic Experience*, 135.
23. Glass-Koentop, *Year of the Moon*, 213.
24. Campanelli, *Wheel of the Year*, 47.
25. Glass-Koentop, *Year of the Moon*, 212.
26. Meadows, *Shamanic Experience*, 135-136.

2

The Tools of
Woodcrafting

In this chapter you will learn which tools are needed for crafting your ritual implements from wood. Keep in mind that the tools described here are always used the same way and for the same purposes, no matter what project you are working on.

Crafting ceremonial objects, such as ritual staffs, from wood is a tradition handed down to contemporary pagans from ancient wise men and women. In constructing such an item, you are making a ritual tool with a thousand-year history and reclaiming its sacred role in religious and magical practices. Today we have the advantage of technologically advanced hardware and tools to help craft our ritual implements, providing us with an easier task and more design options.

The tools listed below are frequently found in households, are inexpensive to purchase, and do not require expertise to use. If you do not own these tools and cannot afford to buy them, many can be rented from businesses that specialize in tool and equipment rental.

Recommended Tools

Chisel

A flat, sharp-edged, metal tool for cutting and shaping wood. It is used to cut grooves and carve designs in wood. To use, hold the beveled side against the wood surface and hit the handle with a hammer.

Clamp

A device used to hold wood pieces together. We recommend the C-clamp, which is inexpensive compared to other clamps and comes in a variety of sizes to suit your needs. The C-clamp has two arms which come together to grip an object firmly. This tool is used to hold the wood in place while working or to hold glued wood pieces together while they dry. The handle is turned to open and close the clamp. Always place small wood blocks between the wood you are working on and the clamp's arms—the firm hold from the metal clamp may dent or damage the wood surface.

Coping Saw

A saw with a narrow blade in a U-shaped frame. It is used for cutting difficult or irregular shapes in the wood and for making curved designs. This tool can also be used for sawing small pieces of wood. To use this saw, push and pull it back and forth to cut the wood.

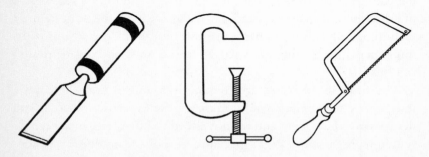

From left to right: Chisel, C-Clamp, Coping Saw.

Crosscut Saw

A saw for cutting wood across the grain. Usually this saw is used only for making straight cuts on wood of all sizes. Apply pressure on the crosscut saw while moving it back and forth.

Electric Drill

An electric tool that comes with a variety of detachable bits, or pointed metal ends, for boring holes in wood and other materials. Drilling is usually done with the drill bit pointing downward into the wood. Use one hand to grip the handle and press the trigger, and the other hand to steady the drill and apply gentle, even pressure while drilling. Proceed carefully and slowly.

Different drills may have different drilling speeds, and most have a switch that changes the drilling direction from forward to reverse.

Note: Wear eye protection when you drill because wood chips and dust will fly into your face. You should wear a face mask to prevent breathing in excessive wood dust. A word of caution: if you do not have a vise attached to a sturdy work table, or other device to securely hold the wood piece while you are drilling, please do not attempt the procedure. Hand held drills can be just as physically harmful as larger, industrial machinery.

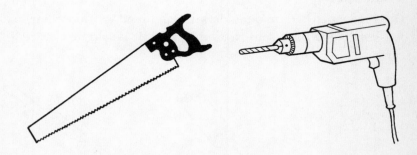

From left to right: Crosscut Saw, Electric Drill.

Elmer's Wood Glue

A glue made by the Borden company for gluing wood projects. While wood glue is yellow in color when it is wet, it dries clear. Standard white Elmer's glue is not suitable for woodcrafting projects, you must use wood glue. While other companies may make wood glue, Elmer's Wood Glue seems to be the most popular brand because of its strength and reliability.

Gouge

A type of chisel with a curved, hollowed blade. A gouge cuts grooves for holes, decoration, and rounded carvings. It is used with a hammer, like a chisel. For delicate carving, use the palm of your hand to hit the top of the handle.

Rasp

A rough file with raised points. A rasp is used as a first step in smoothing the rough surfaces of wood. Hold the rasp with one hand and place the fingers of your other hand on the rasp end to apply pressure. Push the tool in a forward motion only.

A rasp is not an essential tool. We have listed it here because it costs less than a wood plane and works in a similar way. A rasp is also easier to use than a wood plane.

Sandpaper

This is paper coated on one side with sand used for smoothing and polishing wood once construction is done. It is sold in a variety of

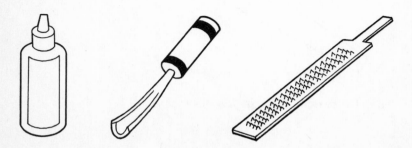

From left to right: Elmer's Wood Glue, Gouge, Rasp.

packs with different grit types—use 80 grit for initial rough sanding, 100 grit for a medium texture, and 250 grit for a smooth surface.

Note: Sand only with the grain, never against the grain. Fold a sheet of sandpaper into a square or cut into 3"x 3" size pieces for better handling. Slide back and forth across the wood in long straight strokes.

Vise

A device consisting of two metal jaws which are opened and closed by a screw or lever. Bolt the vise to a table and use it to hold wood firmly. Different from the C-clamp, the vise is used to keep wood stationary, whereas the C-clamp can be moved about with ease while working.

Note: Always use small wood blocks between the wood and the vise jaws to prevent damage to the wood surface.

Wood Blocks

Small scrap pieces of wood. These are used to protect the wood from damage during use with a clamp or vise. They are placed between the wood surface and the jaws of the vise or clamp.

Wood File

A steel tool with a rough, ridged surface. It is used for smoothing or grinding away wood, shaping wood with irregular curves, removing saw marks, or to flatten knots in the wood. However, it may be used to shape deep, large carvings. Hold the file handle with one hand and

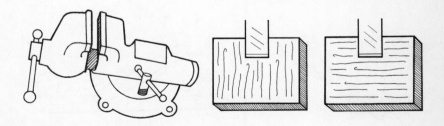

From left to right: Vise, Working with the wood grain, Working against the wood grain.

place the fingers of your other hand on the file end to apply pressure as you move it back and forth.

Wood Plane

This carpenter's tool is used for leveling and smoothing wood. A wood plane has a cutting edge, similar to a knife blade, on its bottom surface. It removes more wood in one stroke than the wood file does. It is also used to make wood straighter or smaller.

The best way to use a plane is to hold it with by the handle in the back and the knob in the front and start at one end or corner of the squared wood. Push in a forward motion while applying slight pressure. Use straight and steady strokes.

Note: Use this device to cut on the edges of wood, with the grain only. Do not cut across the wood grain. Hold the plane's edge against the wood and push in a forward motion only.

Wood Lathe

A wood lathe is a very expensive, professional machine for shaping a piece of wood. Though not essential to crafting the ritual tools presented in this book, if you have access to one it will simplify your project. However, this is a difficult tool to master. A beginner using a wood lathe must have guidance, and a first project on a wood lathe may not come out perfect. A lathe can only work on wood up to 3' or 4' in length and is not ideal for larger projects, such as a ritual staff. The motorized machine holds the wood and turns it rapidly against the edge of a cutting blade or tool. It is used by furniture

From left to right: Wood File, Wood Plane.

manufacturers to create elaborate designs in furniture, make wooden bowls and cups, and to fashion spindle poles. Working with a wood lathe you can produce beautiful wood shapes for your staff or wand.

Additional Tools

Other tools that might be useful in your woodworking projects include cloths to wipe away particles of wood from sanding or carving, and a medium-to-large knife with a non-serrated blade to strip bark from tree branches and to aid in carving. (A Swiss Army knife will do.)

Safety

It is not necessary for you to re-arrange a room in your home into a workshop. You only need a clean, sturdy table to work on. Be sure that the table has been designated as a work table because tools used for your project can scratch surfaces easily; you don't want to damage nice furniture. The table top must be durable and the work area kept free from curious pets and young children. Power tools are of the greatest concern around children; however, it is also possible for them to injure themselves on hand tools, such as chisels, knives, and saws. Keep all such tools away from children.

When working with the chisel, gouge, rasp, wood plane, knife, or drill, please remember to always direct the tool away from you. Failure to do so could cause serious injury.

Safety glasses or goggles should be worn while woodworking. A small piece of wood could fly into your eye during any one of the steps, and result in serious injury. If debris should get into your eye, an eye wash must be applied immediately to the injured eye for removal. If discomfort persists, see your physician.

Always wear a face mask whenever drilling, sawing, or sanding to prevent breathing in wood fibers.

Use common sense and caution during woodworking. Using proper equipment and paying careful attention to instructions will only benefit your work, and your project will be less frustrating.

A Magical Work Space

When undertaking the projects described in this book, it is always best to craft your ritual tools within your sacred space or quiet area. By doing so you will have the privacy and concentration to design your ritual tool and infuse it with your energy and the essence of your spiritual and magical practice. This allows for concentration and communion with your personal deities, who may help you and guide your hands should you become frustrated. Cast your circle and light your favorite incense. Patience and enjoyment are what truly matter. Not everyone is a natural born artist. Your individual artistic designs are what make your ritual tool unique.

3

Ritual Staff Construction and Use

The ritual staff has its roots in antiquity. It was used by the wise, the noble, and the sorcerer and sorceress. All civilizations, religions, and magical orders of ancient eras used a basic staff, whether as an aid for walking, a weapon, or as a symbolic tool in ritual. Staffs from several ancient traditions—Egyptian, Hebrew, Celtic, or early Christian—can be easily recreated for modern use in accordance with your particular magical path.

A ritual staff is crafted to be used for several purposes beyond that of "ritual tool." Its large size allows it to be used in many ways—it can act as a walking stick to assist you in outdoor ventures, as a weapon of defense, and as a versatile ritual implement that can be used throughout your magical-spiritual path. Since it can withstand the wear and tear of being dropped during a ritual, the staff is well suited for frequent outdoor activities and ceremonies. Its design, height, and width should reflect not only cosmetic appeal but also durability.

The most important considerations in designing your ritual staff are to craft one of the best possible wood types for your needs at a height and weight that can be worked with easily during rites, and to construct a ritual tool that will last and is versatile enough to be used in varying environments. The staff, a ritual tool that is both ancient and contemporary, can be used as a limb of your magical-spiritual personage. Its service can reward you for a lifetime.

A Basic Ritual Staff

Materials Needed

To make your ritual staff out of square lumber you will need the following tools and materials:

- Wood stock in the length, width, and thickness that you require
- Elmer's Wood Glue
- Three (or more) C-clamps
- Wood blocks
- Wood plane or rasp
- Sand paper (coarse, medium, and fine grit)
- Vise (optional)
- Wood file (optional)

Determining the Height and Weight of a Basic Ritual Staff

Once you have gathered all tools required for making your ritual staff, first consider the measurements, the design, and the type of material. We strongly suggest that you select your piece of wood using visualization to understand your personal spiritual needs with regard to the ritual staff, along with a tape measure.

The height and thickness of your personal staff is entirely your decision, however it is best that the height is one foot shorter than the individual who will be using it. If you are 5' 7" tall, then your staff should measure approximately 4' 7" in height. If the height of the staff is equal to your own, the staff will be difficult to maneuver and performing any above-the-head movements, such as holding the staff in both hands vertically over your head for the projection of energy, known in Wicca as the magical "Cone of Power," will be physically challenging. A staff that is as tall as you would be unmanageable as well as potentially dangerous to yourself and others.

A short, fat, heavy ritual staff is not recommended either, since its weight would hinder mobility.

If your ritual staff is constructed at half your total height, you then increase the staff's maneuverability, but decrease the ease of holding it while standing. It can be argued that if the staff is half the height of its master, it acts very much like a walking cane. However, we can agree that a staff is easier to use than a cane for regular walking. In addition, the staff has a more majestic, noble presence and appeal.

The weight of your ritual staff is very much determined by your choice of wood, its height, and its thickness. The staff should be at least one inch thick to withstand breakage, but it should not exceed 2½ inches in thickness. Any greater thickness will result in unnecessary weight that may hinder manageability. If your ritual staff is thicker than 2½ inches, it would be like a using a log of firewood for a staff—certainly durable, though not very practical.

A long, skinny staff may easily suffer damage. The staff should be light-weight for easy handling, but the lack of sufficient width to supply needed strength to the wood will result in limited use and eventual breakage. If your staff is made from a dowel, be sure to get a thick one—approximately 2 inches in diameter.

Determine the measurements of the wood you will need before you begin cutting, planing, or sawing away the wood surface.

We recently crafted a ritual staff for a man who is a Wiccan. The gentleman asked us many questions as he tried to determine exactly how his ritual staff should be constructed. He provided us with facts about his height and weight. He also indicated that the staff would be used primarily during outdoor rituals, as he and his fellow Wiccans walked deep into a forest to reach a designated stone circle for their rites. With this information, we knew exactly what type of ritual staff would best suit him.

The client is 6' 4" and weighs 180 pounds. This indicated that the staff should be about 5' 4" tall and 1½ inches thick to support his handling and weight during the walk into the forest and beyond.

Since he is a large man, his ritual staff would certainly require more strength and durability than that of an individual who was 5' 0" tall and weighed 115 pounds. This gentleman would very likely break a ritual staff designed for a smaller individual, and suffer great disappointment. Although he requested that his staff be made from pine or fir, we explained to him that these softwoods would not offer the durability he needed to ensure that his ritual staff would serve him for a very long time. He was not concerned with the magical properties of wood, so he chose elm, an ideal strong hardwood for a substitute wood type. (The gentleman did request that the ritual staff be at least 6' in height, although we felt 5'4" would be more appropriate.)

Another ritual staff we once crafted for an individual is a good example of the importance of determining the measurements of your staff to suit your needs. We made this staff for a woman who followed a Celtic religious tradition. She asked us to make a ritual staff for indoor use only, with very detailed specifications. The height she requested was a foot taller than herself. We advised her before beginning the project that the excessive height of such a staff might do more harm than good due to the difficulty she would experience while using it. She appreciated our concern but assured us that she had considered all possible problems with the height beforehand and that her mind was made up—she wanted an extra-tall staff. Since we were at her service, we agreed to craft her staff just as she wished.

Four weeks after she received her staff, which she had been thoroughly pleased with, she called us in dismay. While casting a circle in the living room of her small apartment, she swung the tall ritual staff into the air. Not only did it destroy the overhead light fixture, the staff itself sustained damage. We offered to provide her with instructions on repairing the staff over the telephone, but the decorations and wood had been damaged beyond repair. Painfully, she recalled our warning and asked that another staff be constructed following our suggested measurements. Her new staff has brought her renewed joy and success in her practice.

We mention this particular example because in making your own staff, you need to consider the area where you will be using it for your magical-spiritual practice. In indoor rituals that involve energy building, especially with other individuals, a staff that is too large can destroy property and potentially cause injury to others.

Determine the Size of Your Wood Piece

You need to decide the length and diameter of your ritual staff before purchasing the wood. Usually length is not a problem. If you have to purchase wood that is too long, the lumber store can cut the wood for you, or you can always cut part of it off.

Diameter (thickness) can be a problem. Commercially sold wood may not be as thick as you desire. If you want a 1½-inch diameter, then the wood must measure 1½" x 1½" in width and thickness.

If the wood purchased is slightly larger in diameter, you can always use a wood plane, wood file, or saw to remove excess wood.

Note: A ritual staff can be constructed from either one piece of wood or two identical pieces of wood. The section beginning on page 38 describes how to do the latter.

Obtaining and Preparing Wood for Your Ritual Staff

ACQUIRING NATURAL WOOD

Acquiring your wood type directly from nature is a highly rewarding learning process. Walking through woodland in search of the tree of your desired wood type requires a book or knowledgeable guide that can identify tree types by bark and leaves. This is a challenge, and one not easily mastered. We have walked through many woodlands and found ourselves confused as to which type of bark is associated with a particular tree. Many barks look similar, as do many leaves. Since tree families have a wide variety of tree types, the search is difficult.

If your home has trees in its yard, this may make your quest easier. If you don't know what type of trees are in your yard, perhaps a neighbor could help identify them. Apartment dwellers may find that the manager of the complex knows what kind of trees are on the property. Be sure to ask your landlord for permission before you start pruning a branch from one of his trees.

Park rangers often know tree types, and it is best to ask them not only what types of trees can be found in the area, but also if you can cut off a branch from a particular tree. Many parks do not allow cutting tree branches or removal of any plant life from the park.

Do not become frustrated when tree hunting. Even in trade schools, woodworking students are not taught how to identify trees. Many professional woodworkers with years of experience still cannot identify a tree without a book or guide. It is a learning process, and you should not think that the identification of various tree types is common knowledge to most woodworking professionals.

Obtaining your wood from nature will give you a more natural-looking staff. Tree branches, often filled with worm holes, knots, and markings from the elements, are particularly well-suited for making naturalistic staffs and wands. Your local forest or woodland often provides more choices in wood type than are generally available at commercial lumberyards.

Step 1   *Obtaining your tree branch.*

You should look for a branch that is already broken from the tree. Since freshly cut wood must be dried before use, taking an already dried branch would save you time and save an intact branch from being needlessly cut. However, a fallen branch must be tested for rot before you plan to use it. Use a saw, knife, or ax to gently cut bark away, then cut a thin strip of wood off the branch. If the wood is rotten, it may be very dry and will fall apart easily. Rotten wood may also be wet or weak, have black color on the surface, and be easily broken in two by your bare hands.

If a fallen branch cannot be found in good condition, then a fresh branch should be cut. A good, healthy branch has firm bark and should be hard to cut. The bark should not come off easily and the branch should resist breaking in two. It should have no excessive black pigment on the surface once the bark is removed. (The only exception to this rule is ebony, a wood not commonly found in North America.) Never cut more branch than you need. The branch can be cut with an ax, hatchet, large knife, or saw.

All of this should be carried out with an attitude of respect toward nature. The process should be done by first asking the tree's permission to remove the branch, letting the tree know what will become of its use, and then giving thanks once the branch is severed.

As humans, we often assume that nature is here for our taking. It is more than likely that the tree you choose has lived much longer than you and has much wisdom. Your use of the tree's wood is a privilege, not a right. It is a gift from nature to you, given without question. Always give reverence and thanks for the use of the wood, and its wisdom and energies from within. We always leave a gift for the tree in return—two silver coins or a generous bowl of water poured at its roots.

Step 2   *Removing the bark.*
Once you have your branch, the next step is to peel the bark away, exposing the underlying wood. You can use your bare hands to remove the bigger pieces and a knife to remove the rest. It is better to remove the bark outside since all kinds of surprises may lie underneath: insect larvae, ants, mites, and many other creatures.

Step 3   *Examining your wood.*
After the bark is removed, examine the wood's surface. Healthy wood normally feels moist to the touch and has a faint odor that is pleasant and fresh. If the wood has dirt particles or debris, wipe the surface with a damp paper towel or cloth.

Do not use excessive amounts of water—the wood's surface and water are natural enemies. While examining the wood, you may see worm holes from various insects and their larvae, or knots—hard lumps on the wood where a tree branch would have grown. (Instructions in Step 5 deal with this problem.)

Step 4   *Drying the wood.*

Before you begin carving, painting, staining, and other work, it is important to let the wood dry thoroughly to prevent future rot and to prepare the wood surface to be worked. When wood is wet or moist, it expands and presents many problems for woodworking. Moist wood pores will absorb stain, paint, and finishes incorrectly and cause the stain to seep into cracks or appear smudged. Once the wood has dried properly, it will shrink and become very easy to work with.

To dry the wood, simply place it in a dry area where it will not be disturbed by rain, a "chew-happy" pet, or possible damage. We have placed drying wood against a wall beside a heat radiator or leaned it against a kitchen counter to dry from the heat of a nearby stove. Placing the wood under a window is a good idea, since the sunlight and incoming fresh air will speed the drying process.

It is difficult to explain precisely how to determine if a piece of wood is completely dry. When the wood is dry, the surface will appear distinctly lighter in color and feel dryer to the touch than when you found it. Usually a week in a warm area is enough drying time, unless the wood came from a climate with excessive rainfall. Let the staff dry for at least a week or two and examine it occasionally for dryness and insect larvae.

Step 5   *Dealing with wood parasites.*

Parasites should not cause any worry. Most are removed when the bark is stripped. If there are small areas where parasites are seen during the drying process, dip a clean cloth in diluted bleach (we suggest a dilute mixture of ½ cup of bleach to 3 cups of water), and remove excess water from the cloth so it is not dripping wet, and gently wipe the area. Should an area of the wood's surface be darkly discolored or otherwise accidentally stained, this method will also lighten the surface and remove the stain. Any worm holes may be filled later with wood filler (see chapter 9).

Step 6   *Finishing touches.*

When the wood is dry, you may able to craft it to your specifications. Unlike commercially acquired wood, sanding to obtain a round shape is unnecessary. Unless you prefer a smoother surface, sanding can be avoided.

Acquiring Commercial Wood

Step 1   *Determine your wood type.*

Should you choose to create your ritual staff from commercially purchased wood, you must first decide on the type of wood you would like to use. Many lumber stores do not have an extensive selection in stock—the demand for some types of wood is low since they are not used in commercial or furniture manufacturing, while others are too costly. Lumber and hardware stores usually carry various types of pine, poplar, redwood, oak, and birch, though some stores will have a wider selection. Call or visit a few to see if they carry your choice. In some cases, out-of-stock wood may be ordered. However, large orders are usually required, and that is not a realistic choice for a small project like a staff.

Cabinet-making shops may have wood types that are difficult to obtain at lumber or hardware stores and might sell you a strip of wood or some scrap wood that is large enough for your project.

Step 2   *Decide between "round stock" and square lumber.*

Lumber is sold "squared in width." If you desire an already rounded wood piece, lumber stores have dowels, or "round stock" on hand, in different sizes. Usually the types of wood, as well as the range of diameters from which to choose, are limited when buying round stock. Some may prefer a perfectly round staff—in this case a commercial wood dowel is the obvious answer, and it will greatly simplify construction of the staff.

Many people prefer their staffs to have a more unique and natural "rough" look achieved by starting with a square piece of wood that is rounded, carved, or filed into a staff that is somewhat rounded, yet rugged-looking. This method is described on the following pages.

Using Two Pieces of Wood For Your Ritual Staff

If the thickness of the wood available to you is slightly less than you would like, one solution is to purchase two pieces of your wood type and glue them together to achieve the desired diameter.

Step 1   *Obtain two pieces of square wood.*
You can purchase an extra long piece of wood and cut the length in half. This will give you two pieces to glue together to obtain your desired diameter. To determine the thickness of each piece you will buy, divide your diameter in half. For example, if you want your staff to have a diameter of 2 inches, then each piece of wood should measure at least 1 inch in thickness.

Step 2   *Apply glue.*
The process of gluing is simple. You need Elmer's Wood Glue, at least three C-clamps, and wood blocks to protect the surface of the ritual item from the jaws of the clamps.

Examine your wood. Make sure it is clean of all dirt and foreign matter. Use a dry cloth to wipe any debris away. This will ensure good bonding. Apply the glue generously to one side of each piece of wood. Spread the glue evenly with a piece of scrap wood or your fingers. Do not leave any bare spots, doing so could result in poor bonding.

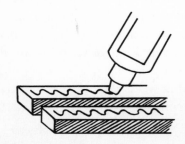

Step 2. Apply Elmer's Wood Glue generously to both pieces of wood. Spread it evenly across each piece of wood.

Step 3   *Align the two pieces.*

Once you have applied the glue, join the glued surfaces and line up their edges so they meet evenly.

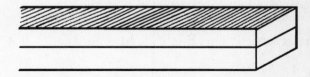

Step 3. Align the two pieces of wood, glued sides facing each other.

Step 4   *Apply wood clamps.*

First lay your ritual staff on the floor or a table. Be sure to use wood blocks, wood scraps, or a thin, hardcover book in between your ritual item and the clamp jaws. Failure to do so will result in damage to your project.

Use clamps properly and space them appropriately. It is best to place clamps at each end of the wood on both sides and clamps every foot inward, depending on length of your staff. Put clamps in place over the wood blocks and tighten them from the middle to the ends of the staff. This places an equal amount of pressure to all areas of the wood. Tighten until you notice glue oozing from between the wood pieces. Do this with each clamp.

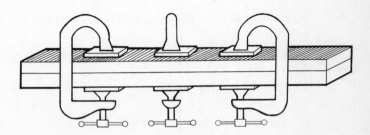

Steps 4–5. Align the two pieces of wood and use C-clamps placed at the center and both ends of the wood. Tighten them and allow the glue to dry thoroughly.

Step 5 *Let the glue dry.*

Leave the staff clamped and undisturbed for at least twenty-four hours, allowing it to dry. After glue has dried, remove the clamps. Remove the excess glue by scraping it off with a chisel, wood plane, or wood file.

Constructing the Basic Ritual Staff

Step 1 *Shaping your staff.*

Decide how you would like your ritual staff to be shaped. If you purchased the wood squared, you may desire it rounded. If you know someone with a wood lathe, you might ask them if they can show you how to use it or can round your wood for you.

Step 2 *Rounding your staff.*

The easiest way to achieve a round staff is to draw a circle in pencil at each end of the wood the same diameter as you'd like your finished staff. This will act as a guide for you to follow when cutting.

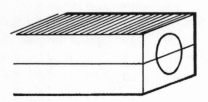

Step 2. Pencil a circle at each end of your wood to act as a guide for shaping your staff.

Step 3 *Secure the staff for rounding.*

Use a vise or clamps to secure the staff in a horizontal position. A vise is beneficial since it allows both of your hands the freedom to work.

Step 4 *Choose tools for rounding.*

A wood plane is an excellent tool to use for rounding. A rasp can be used in place of a wood plane, but it will take longer to achieve roundness. Use your penciled circles to guide you and begin. Do not frustrate yourself by attempting to attain perfect roundness. You can round just the ends, or the entire staff. You can create a "curvy" shape by applying excessive pressure on different areas of the wood surface. Instructions on the proper way to use a wood plane are given in chapter 2.

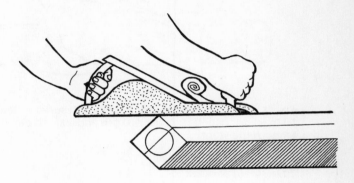

Step 4. Use a wood plane to easily remove excess wood and to begin shaping your staff into a round object.

Step 5   *Determine if sanding is required.*
Sanding is recommended if you would like to stain, finish, or enamel your staff. A refined appearance and an even application of stain, enamel, or other finish can only be achieved when the wood surface has been sanded. Without sanding, the pigment of the stain will dry to a darker shade and splintering, scratches, or flaws are visible. However, some people feel these irregularities make the wood look more natural than sanding it completely smooth. Use your discretion.

Step 6   *Sanding your staff.*
Sanding should be done from top to bottom, and with the grain. Sanding against the grain will cause more scratches and abrasions on the surface. Begin with 60 to 80 grit sandpaper. This will sand away big scratches and flaws caused by

the wood's natural texture or by the use of a wood plane, file, or rasp. Then use a 100 grit paper, which will eliminate small flaws. Finally, apply 150 grit sandpaper. This sands the wood's surface to a silky smoothness. No flaws can be seen or felt after proper sanding.

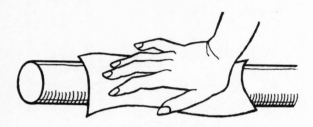

Step 6. Sand your staff to create a smooth surface. Begin with 60 or 80 grit paper, then use 100 grit and 150 grit papers to smooth the wood.

Step 7   *Finishing touches.*

Once your ritual staff is rounded to your liking, you can carve, paint, or wood brand it. Make sure you carve and wood brand before sanding. Painting should be done after sanding.

Since your ritual staff is your personal tool, there are no set procedures of decoration to follow. (see chapter 8: "Carving, Painting, and Wood Branding.") Now is the time for you to infuse the ritual staff with your own energies, and penetrate it with the power of your personal symbols. Let your creativity flow!

The following two ritual staff patterns, the Shaman Rattle Staff and the Sword Staff, require only the tools listed below, along with patience and faith in yourself.

The Shaman Rattle Staff

The Shaman Rattle Staff is a fairly easy tool for a beginner to construct. This staff produces a rattling sound that aids meditation and creates a rhythm for dancing or chanting.

Materials Needed

The following is a list of tools needed for this project:

- Commercial wood: Two 3' long pieces measuring 1" thick by 2" wide (many lumber yards will cut your wood to the exact measurements you need)

Or

- Naturally acquired wood: One piece that should measure 3' in length and 2" in width

- C-clamp or vise

- Chisel or gouge

- Elmer's Wood Glue

- Ruler or yard stick

- Sand papers: 100, 150, 200 (or 240) grit

- Hand or power saw

- Wood plane

- Wood file

Step 1   *Obtain two equal pieces of wood.*

If you are using naturally acquired wood, cut the 3' long piece in half, down the center of its length. This will give you a flattened surface on one side of each separate 3' long piece of the branch for the staff interior.

If you are using commercial wood, you should have two three-foot long pieces of wood that are two inches wide and one inch thick.

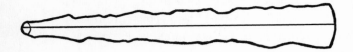

Step 1. If you use naturally acquired wood, cut the three-foot piece in half, down the center of its length.

Step 2   *Cut the center grooves.*

For the next step you may use a chisel, gouge, carving tool, table saw, or a router (a handheld rotary power tool useful in making designs on edges of wood or grooves in the wood). Use a pencil and a ruler to sketch a line to follow. Carefully cut out a lengthwise groove down the center of both pieces of wood. (This groove goes on the flat, interior side for those using a natural wood.) Leave at least ½" of wood on either side of the groove. Stop the groove at least 6" before the bottom of your staff. You do not want the groove to end at the bottom of both pieces of the wood. If you do, no pebbles or rattle-makers can be held inside the hollow interior of the staff. The groove must be made on both pieces of your wood.

It is also important that the groove does not go through to the exterior side of the wood. The groove will hold small stones, beads, pebbles, or whatever rattle makers you choose. It must be wide and deep enough so these items will move freely inside, causing a rattling noise. (diagram 2, page 45).

Step 2. Cut a center groove, but be careful to leave at least 6 inches before the end of the wood.

Step 3   *Applying glue.*

After carving the grooves, apply Elmer's Wood Glue down either side of the groove on both pieces of wood. Apply four lines of glue along the complete length of both wood pieces. Be generous in your application, but do not allow glue to collect in the groove. If any should seep into the groove, simply wipe it away with a cloth. Do not worry about any small traces left behind.

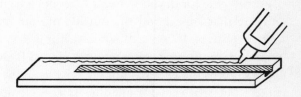

Step 3. Apply glue to both pieces of wood, taking care not to let any drip into the center groove.

Step 4   *Clamping.*

Once the wood glue has been generously applied, place the two pieces of wood together. Make sure that you have the two bottom ends where the groove stopped glued together. The two grooves should now appear as a hole at the top end of your staff (diagram 4, page 46). Try to adjust the grooves to meet equally. When you press the two pieces firmly together, use C-clamps or a vise to hold the wood securely in place. Remember to place scrap pieces of wood between your staff and the clamp or vise jaws.

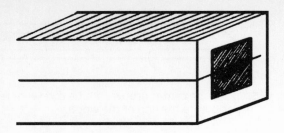

Step 4. Align the grooves of the two pieces of wood, press the planks together firmly, and use C-clamps or a vise to hold the wood in place.

The staff must be left undisturbed in its hold for at least one day. Since you applied a generous amount of glue, it may take longer than overnight to dry thoroughly.

Step 5 *Testing for dryness.*
Test the glue for dryness after 24 hours by feeling any glue residue that appears on the outside of your staff between the two halves. If you are certain that it is dry, unclamp the staff and gently try to separate the pieces. If they separate, even slightly, the glue has not dried sufficiently. Apply more glue where the halves pulled apart and clamp them back into drying position.

Step 6 *Rounding your staff.*
After the glue has thoroughly dried, leave the wood in its hold if you used a vise instead of C-clamps. If you have used commercially purchased wood, take your wood plane or wood file and begin planing away at the surface to shape the wood into desired roundness. Shaping in this case refers to giving a circular diameter to the staff. This is also an ideal time to smooth any extremely rough end edges or splintered areas. Commercial wood will require more work, since it has squared edges. This step will remove any glue that oozed between the wood halves and is visible on your staff's surface. This is an important step because when you later paint, stain, finish, or carve, you do not want glue or rough spots getting in your way.

Step 7   *Choosing your "rattle-makers."*
After you've completed the construction of the staff, you
need to choose small rocks, pebbles, or beads to drop inside
the ritual staff. Make sure they are smaller than the width of
the hollow interior or entrance. Do not place so many
objects inside that they collect up to the entrance. You want
these objects to move freely and rattle. Place some items
inside, hold your thumb over the top end entrance, shake
the staff, and see if the sound you desire has been created.

Many objects work as rattle makers. A large quantity of dried
cactus needles will produce a "raining" sound. B-B gun pel-
lets and lead fishing weights also work well. Tiny bells sold at
craft stores may produce a truly musical sound. Experiment
with different objects to acquire a sound you like.

Step 8   *Sealing the top of the staff.*
The last step is to cork the open
entrance. Place a small amount of
craft glue inside on the entrance
walls, and stick a long perfect-fit-
ting crystal, slice of amethyst, or
other stone into the opening.
After the glue around the chosen
entrance cap has dried, your interior rattle-makers cannot escape
and your staff will look very nice.

Go ahead and flip your staff
upside-down. Shake it. Can you
hear the objects inside rattle and
move together musically?

Step 8. Seal the top
of your Shaman
Rattle Staff with a
perfectly fitting
crystal.

The exterior of your staff can now
be carved, painted, wood branded, or designed to your preference. If you decide to carve, please be very careful not to
carve too deeply and reach the hollow interior of your staff,
or too forcefully, which may unlock the glue's durable hold.

◆   ◆   ◆

Sword Staff

The Sword Staff is similar to antique
cane swords. Like the cane sword, it
contains a metal sword blade hidden in
the staff. This is a project for the
advanced craftsperson, since it not only
works with wood but requires skillful
measuring, cutting, and gluing, and working with a metal sword blade. We strongly
advise that you do not make a sword staff as
your first project.

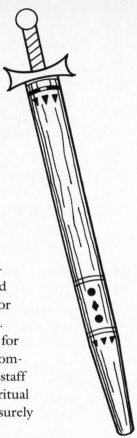

Cane swords are fascinating and unusual
hidden weapons from decades past that still
captivate people today. Making your own is a
challenge, but the reward is well worth it. Perhaps hundreds of years from now, your sword
staff may be passed from collector to collector
and end up as a treasured display in a museum.

What is unique about this project is that for
some religious and magical practitioners it com-
bines two ritual tools into one instrument: the staff
and the sword, or athame. If you use both ritual
tools in your practice, this convenience will surely
enhance your ritual activity.

We've tried to make these instructions as simple as
possible. Since they are difficult, you should read them
thoroughly before proceeding.

Note: Owning a sword staff may be illegal in your area, as it can be
considered a concealed weapon. You may wish to investigate these laws
before creating this tool.

Materials Needed

- You need all the same tools and materials used in the Shaman
  Rattle Staff.
- A sword

Step 1   *Obtain a sword.*

New sword blades are tricky to obtain. Try searching antique shops or flea markets for a blade, or purchase a sword and use it as is. There is no sense in taking a sword apart—you will need the handle.

Purchasing a sword at an antique dealer can be expensive. They usually cost between $100 and $600 dollars. There are other options. If you have a local historical society, you might ask them if they know of a blacksmith. Though not common today, there are still a few practicing blacksmiths and some will know the art of "sword-smithing." Garage sales in affluent neighborhoods or New Age shops may surprise you with swords available for sale.

For other commercial sources that carry swords and blades, see the Resources Guide on page 213.

Step 2   *Obtain your wood.*

Once you find your sword or sword blade you need to obtain commercial or naturally acquired wood. Separate the wood into two identical pieces as described in the instructions for the Shaman Rattle Staff.

Step 3   *Cut the center grooves.*

The only difference between this step and Step 2 of the Shaman Rattle Staff is that your groove must be engraved to fit your sword blade precisely. This is tricky. The sword blade should fit snugly, but be able to be drawn smoothly from the staff.

Lay the sword blade on the interior section of your wood pieces to pencil an outline of the blade for a guide as you carve [diagram 3(a), page 50].

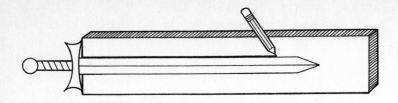

Step 3(a). Carefully trace the outline of your sword blade on the wood.

The groove must be the same shape as your sword blade. For this reason, it is best to acquire your blade first, then your wood, so that you can determine what size wood you will need. Remember to leave at least six inches of solid wood at the bottom of your staff. If the blade tip is too close to the bottom, in time it could break through the staff. [diagram 3(b)]

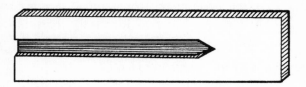

Step 3(b). Cut the groove to the exact dimensions of your sword blade.

Step 4   *Gluing, clamping, and drying.*
These processes are the same as those of the Shaman Rattle Staff. When you prepare to glue your wood halves together, do not leave the sword blade between them. The glue could seep into the groove and glue your blade to the wood, forcing you to saw the staff apart to remove it. C-clamp the wood together or place the wood in a vise to dry overnight. Once you are certain the glue is dry, remove the glue that has seeped outside the seams of the two wood halves.

Step 5   *Testing to check blade fit.*

Try placing your blade into the sheath. It should be slightly snug, but slide in with gentle pressure. In time, as the sword is pulled out and pushed in, it will loosen the fit as the blade wears away excess interior wood to create a perfect alignment.

If the blade will not slide in with gentle pressure, or it feels as if the sheath will break, then your measurements were incorrect or excess glue pooled into the groove and is blocking the entrance. Do not panic. Take a long, thin, pointed object, such as a wire clothes hanger that has been taken apart, and slide it into the sheath. If there is definite blockage, try scraping with the clothes hanger until the glue finally gives.

If there is no blockage and you are certain the measurements are misaligned, you can try gluing rough sand paper to the clothes hanger, then sticking it inside the sheath to rub the interior—hopefully widening the grooves. Be sure that the sandpaper is attached well to the clothes hanger. If the sand paper falls off inside the staff, use the clothes hanger to fish it out. The only other solution is to get an electric drill, attach a very long drill bit, and drill away the wood inside. In the end, if you cannot get the blade to fit inside, you may have to start the project over.

Step 6   *Finishing and decorating the sheath.*

If your sword already has a handle, you can now begin decorating the staff itself. Again, follow the same steps as for the Shaman Rattle Staff, rounding the edges if necessary. If carving, be careful not to break the glue's hold.

Making a Sword Handle or "Grip"

If you acquired only a sword blade, you will need to construct a handle for it. You can make the handle out of wood by using two square pieces of wood cut to your specifications.

Step 1   *Cutting gouges for the tang.*

Take a pencil and trace the tang (the top projecting prong or point that fits into the handle) on each piece of wood, in the center, leaving at least an inch of solid wood at the top end. Most blades have holes for pins or screws in their tangs. You do not have to go to the trouble of drilling holes in your wood handle to place pins or screws. After penciling the tang onto the wood pieces, use a chisel or gouge to cut out the imprint. Each imprint should be cut to half the thickness of the tang.

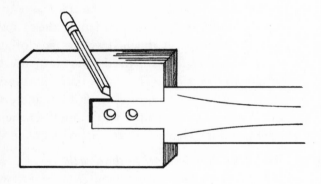

Step 1. Trace the tang of your blade to a wood block.

Step 2   *Fitting and gluing.*

Place the tang between the wood pieces. The wood pieces, with the tang between them, should fit together perfectly. Use a wood plane or file to create a rough surface on either side of the interior wood. This provides a good foundation for the glue to adhere to the wood. Apply a generous amount of Elmer's Wood Glue all around the imprints and inside the grooves. Since the wood glue may not adhere well to the metal tang, you may wish to ask your home center or hardware store for a small bottle of epoxy or other glue that adheres well to metal, and use that inside the tang imprints.

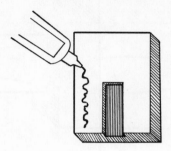

Step 2. Apply wood glue to the wood block. Select an epoxy or other glue that adheres well to metal and use that in the channel you've created for the blade tang.

Step 3 *Clamping.*

Put the tang between the wood pieces and place the wood in a C-clamp or vise to dry overnight. Remember to place wood blocks between your handle and the jaws of the C-clamp or vise. Although the glue may dry overnight, it is best to allow the wood to set for a couple of days before shaping the handle, just to be certain it is dry and durable.

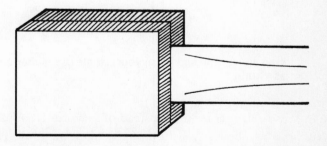

Step 3. Place to blocks together with the tang in between. Clamp and allow to dry thoroughly.

Step 4   *Shaping and finishing your handle.*

After the wood has set, pencil the desired outline of your handle on the wood [diagram 4(a)].

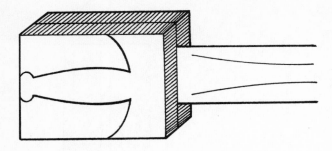

Step 4(a). Use a pencil to trace the outline of your handle on the wood blocks.

After you are satisfied with your sketch, carefully begin sawing or carving away the excess wood. Add any decoration desired to your handle [diagram 4(b)].

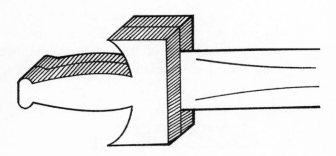

Step 4(b). Shape and finish your handle using your pencil tracing as a guide.

You may use a dagger or knife instead of a sword. If so, use the same instructions as above. A store-bought blade or knife is sufficient because it will be infused with your energies and creativity when you make your staff.

Your sword, knife, or dagger may slip out of the staff if held by its handle. It is better to hold the staff just below its handle while conducting any activity, such as walking, with your personal staff.

Crafting a sword staff is a difficult project, even for experienced woodcrafters. Don't get discouraged if your first attempt does not succeed. Practice and patience are the keys.

Ritual Staff Use

The ritual staff is a primary ritual tool that plays diverse roles in spiritual and magical workings. It literally accompanies you during every phase in ritual. Perhaps this is best shown by examining the various stages in ritual when the staff is used.

In the next several pages, we will discuss many ritual techniques employed in the Wiccan religion, particularly those which involve the use of a ritual staff. Many of the elements found in these rituals are common to other spiritual and magical paths as well.

Circle Casting

In casting a circle you are creating sacred space to set the environment (indoors or outdoors) off from the physical plane and enter the realm between the worlds. You create a safe sanctuary where you can practice your religious and magical work fully loved and validated. The circle is the safe and confidential space created to hold communion with the divine. To be within the circle is to be in the presence of your deity(s) and to be between the realms of earth and universe.[1]

In ritualistic circle casting, the staff's top end should be pointed to the earth, or to the floor, when outlining the circle's boundary. The reason for this is that the staff's primary objective is to channel power. Your personal power, interfacing with the energies from the tree within the wooden staff, is channeled through the staff's structure, then directed and expelled from the top end. For ritual staffs that have a crystal, amethyst, precious stone, or symbolic top ornament, you will point the top ornament to the ground.

The art of circle casting is an ancient practice. A Roman ambassador in a foreign country would draw a circle around himself with his staff to show he should be safe from attack; the Babylonians drew a circle of flour on the floor around the bed of a sick individual to keep demons away; German Jews in the Middle Ages would draw a circle around the bed of a woman in labor to protect her from evil spirits.[2] The circle not only keeps unwanted energies out, it also keeps the wanted magical energy—the raised power—in.[3]

This procedure differs from the act of grounding after a powerful ritual. In grounding, the bottom end of the staff is held firmly to the ground as the earth absorbs the overflow of energies produced by the ritual. This allows your energy level to return to normal after magical rites.

Every magical-spiritual path has its own formula for circle casting or setting aside sacred space. Here, we will examine the Wiccan religion's technique for casting a circle using the ritual staff.

In Wicca, the drawing of the circle starts in either the east or in the north. The direction is used depends on what particular Wiccan tradition one follows. Here, we will focus on beginning in the east.

Starting in the east, the circle is drawn clockwise. (There are exceptions where the circle is drawn counterclockwise.) The circle is cast by visualization that is enhanced by a physical gesture made with the staff or casting tool.[4] Trace the circumference of the circle by holding the staff in both hands, with the top end pointed to the ground as you slowly walk clockwise. If you are holding the ritual outdoors, the circle is actually marked upon the earth's soil as you walk its circumference.

In this first phase of casting the circle, you only need to outline the circle once with the staff. By holding the staff in both hands with a firm and steady grip, you will infuse the staff with your personal power. This power can be directed and projected out of the staff's top onto the ground, outlining the circle's circumference. Afterward, you may choose to retrace the circle with incense, salt and water, or other substance, to purify the circle.

The circle may also be cast symbolically by standing in the center and sweeping the staff in a clockwise direction, casting outward from the circle's middle.[5] The sweep is done once from left to right.

It is reasonable to state that here is the place within the ritual where an elegant and elaborately decorated ritual staff adds much to the beauty, visualization, and magical effect of creating a sacred boundary.[6] The physical procedure of circle casting is the same whether using the staff, finger, hand, wand, or athame (ritual knife). However, the knowledge that you have created the staff, a ritual implement universally used in ancient times, as well as a tool that contains a natural life force from the plant realm, will certainly add magical vitality and divine energy to your rites.

Calling the Elements

The second step in the ritual provides another opportunity to use your staff. Calling of the elements requires you to invite, not demand, the presence of the Earth, Air, Fire, and Water elements. The purpose of this is to call upon the forces of nature in order to conduct devotional rites or practice magic. Each element has certain characteristics that are needed for the performance of natural magic or reverential ceremonies. In certain pagan religions, calling the elements signifies recognition and respect for the cosmic forces and universal powers of creation. If you are conducting a healing ritual or some other form of magic, you petition the elements for additional energy to help in the process.

Candles or other objects are placed to mark the four directions and their corresponding elements (east-Air, south-Fire, west-Water, north-Earth). After the circle is cast, the candles are lit and each element is introduced beginning with Air in the east. With one or both hands, whichever grip is most comfortable for you, hold the staff horizontally over each candle with the top of the staff pointing away from you and toward the specific direction.

In the Ink Mountain Coven, the priest or priestess conducts this procedure by standing at the appropriate direction, vertically raising the staff safely above the lit candle with the top facing the sky. The theory is that the force of the element penetrates the top of the staff and permeates the priest or priestess as the energy travels down the staff and exits, now invited and present, through the staff's bottom end. For the rest of the rite, the elemental energy remains in, or near, its designated direction candle.[7] Again, you must perform this technique in a way that is most comfortable for you.

Once the staff is in position for calling the element, you may choose to speak sacred words of introduction for each of the four elements. Visualization should accompany this procedure. Colors of smoke or light rays are often visualized during each invocation of an element. This will assist you in sensing each element's entry and presence in your circle. You may choose your own colors for the elements, but many religious or magical paths use a set color for each.

The following is our version of the calling of the elements.

Beginning in the east with the element of Air, state the following while visualizing the white color of pure, clean air:

> *Element of the east; that of Air; I invite thy presence into our temple. May thy strong winds of a tempest destroy all negativity that might reside within our circle, and may thy refreshing, gentle breezes fill our lungs with life.*

Walking from the eastern candle and carrying the ritual staff, approach the southern candle. Hold the staff horizontally in your right hand, with its top end pointing away from you, over the southern candle. Call the element of the south while visualizing the red-orange color of Fire:

> *Element of the south; that of Fire; I invite thy presence into our temple. May thy burning fires banish all evil, and may we feel the warmth of thine energy.*

Next, walk to the west and call the element of Water. Holding the staff horizontally in your right hand, point the top end of the staff away from you, above the designated western candle and visualize the sparkling, deep blue-green of pure water:

> *Element of the west; that of Water; I invite thy presence into our temple. May thy salted waters wash away all negativity within our temple and may we bathe in thine essence.*

Finally, approach the northern candle. Hold the staff horizontally in your right hand with its top end pointed away from you. Invite the element of Earth, visualizing the rich, dark brown color of fertilized soil:

Element of the north; that of Earth; I invite thy presence into our temple. May thine energies erode the negativity within this temple and may thy soil sustain life and healing for all who reside upon it.

Within a coven, the priest or priestess may call all the elements, or divide the four elements between them. At times, other coven members may be chosen to call the elements. If this is the case, one ritual staff may be used and passed to each person calling an element, or all may have their own staffs.

Invoking Deity

The next step is the calling of the God and Goddess. Hold the staff vertically in one or both hands high above your head, pointing the top of staff toward the heavens. Summon your deity(s) by saying sacred words, such as the following invocation to the Goddess:

Great Mother (Goddess) of all creatures, I ask that Thou grace this ritual with Thy presence. Lend us Thy knowledge of divinity and of the eternal Wheel of Life. I welcome Thee to our temple for reverence and communion.

Although it is not necessary, you may visualize the deity. Some people visualize their deity descending from heaven and standing before them, within their circle. Many visualize a golden light touching the top of the staff—the light trickles down the length of the staff and is absorbed into the body of the priest or priestess. Visualize the energy of the deity in whatever manner appeals to and works best for you.

The invocation of your God is carried out in a similar way. Holding your staff in the same manner as you did while calling the Goddess, invoke by stating:

Father of all creatures, my Lord, whose Sun rises and sets in the ceaseless Circle of Life, I ask that Thou grace this ritual with Thy presence. Allow me the lessons of Thy divine wisdom. I welcome Thee to our temple for reverence and communion.

If your ritual practice include some aspects of ceremonial magic, you may or may not invoke deities, but rather evoke entities to assist in magical work. The concepts are the same, although many magical orders have their own instructions for invocation and evocation.

Drawing Down the Moon

The staff also plays a significant role in those rituals performed during the Full Moon. Solitary practitioners or covens of Goddess-oriented religions practice Full Moon rituals in order to commune with the Goddess, draw the power of the Full Moon or Goddess from the universe down to the earth-plane, and draw it into oneself—to become the Goddess.[8] The reason for conducting such a procedure is not only to give reverence to the Goddess, but to have her power within, and use it to aid one's magical work.

Within most covens, the priestess traditionally conducts the drawing down of the Moon and invokes the power of the Goddess. A priest can certainly do this as well, with the same positive effect.

Generally, religions in the Craft use the same ritual techniques to draw down the Moon for covens and solitary practitioners alike. The following is a generic ritual for drawing down the Moon suitable for both solitary and group work.

The ritual is conducted either outdoors or at a window facing the Moon. If weather conditions do not permit this, then you should use lighted candles as symbols of the Goddess' moonlight (as in the ritual given below). The preparation, circle casting, and the calling of the elements is conducted beforehand.

Invoking a pentacle.

Standing straight with your feet comfortably apart, and holding the staff in one or both hands, point your staff's top end toward the white candle, which represents the Goddess.

Carefully, above the candle flame, trace an invoking pentagram. (Should the Moon be visible, you would trace the pentagram "over the Moon.")

Then bring the staff to an upright position with its top facing upward. Lean the staff toward your chest and allow the top to touch your heart. Recite sacred words to draw down the Moon:

I invoke the power of my Goddess; known by countless names of the ancient. Diane, Isis, Selene.

I invoke, O Goddess, thy power so graciously lent for my magical work. Know that this power is revered and respected. May this sacred power now enter and live within me.

Visualization is often done to symbolically draw the power into your being. A golden stream of light can be pictured, extending down from the Moon or candle flame to the staff and absorbed into your being.

The main magical work may be conducted thereafter, and in some pagan religions a recited Charge of the Goddess is spoken by the practitioner as if he or she were the Goddess.

Ritual Invocation

Ritual invocation is a declaration to the divine about the purpose of the ritual being conducted. Once all deities have been invoked, the practitioner remains standing in the circle and thumps the bottom end of the staff on the floor or ground. This symbolically calls the attention of the divine presence as the practitioner recites a short description of the events that take place during the remainder of the ritual. The following is an example:

On this night I summoned Thee for the purpose of reverence and celebration of the Great Sabbat of the Spring Equinox. Mother Earth has awakened and now is the time of birth, growth, and renewal. We come together on this night to celebrate the Wheel of the Year's turning of Spring.

Thump the staff on the ground once again. Events of the ritual may then commence.

Imbolc Ritual

The following version of the Imbolc Sabbat ritual for a Wiccan coven illustrates the use of two wooden staffs during a ritual. The entire ceremony is lengthy. Therefore, we've included only those portions of the ritual that employ the ritual staff.

Imbolc takes place on February 2 of the Wheel of the Year. It signifies the recovery of the Goddess after giving birth to the God. The warming weather and lengthening periods of sunlight awaken her after winter. This Sabbat signifies purification after the dormancy of winter and celebrates the renewing power of the Sun, (symbolic of the God). Imbolc is also known as the Feast of Pan or Brigid's Day (in the Celtic tradition). It is a festival of light and fertility.

The altar is adorned with symbols of the season—white flowers, or perhaps snow held in a dish. The orange candles upon the altar are lit; they illuminate the sacred circle as the scent of cinnamon and musk incense drifts through the air. After preparation, the calling of the elements, and the opening phases of the Imbolc Ritual, the coven members arrange themselves around the circle facing inward. The High Priest stands with his back to the altar. The High Priestess faces him.

With his right hand the High Priest takes the staff, which has been leaning against the altar. A smaller, phallic staff lies on the altar, which the High Priest takes into his left hand and assumes the Osiris position (holding the shafts of respective tools in his clenched fists—his wrists are crossed and the shafts cross above his wrists).

The High Priestess, facing the High Priest as he stands before the altar, invokes the God into him by saying:

> *Dread Lord of Death and Resurrection,*
> *Of Life, and the Giver of Life,*
> *Lord within ourselves, whose name is Mystery of Mysteries,*
> *Encourage our hearts,*
> *Let Thy Light crystallize itself in our blood,*
> *Fulfilling of us resurrection;*
> *For there is no part of us that is not of the Gods.*
> *Descend, we pray Thee, upon Thy servant and priest.*[9]

The High Priest places the phallic staff back onto the altar, raises his right hand holding the other staff so that its top points into the air, and draws the Invoking Pentagram of Earth in the air toward the High Priestess as he says, "Blessed be."

Then the High Priest steps to one side while the High Priestess and the women of the coven prepare "Brigid's Bed." They lay the biddy (a foot-long gathering of straw with a straw crosspiece for arms, dressed in doll-sized women's clothing) and the phallic staff side-by-side in the center of the circle with their top ends toward the altar.[10] Next, they place lighted candlesticks on either side of the ceremonial bed. The High Priestess and her women stand round the bed, together saying:

> *Brid is come—Brid is welcome!*
> *Brid is come—Brid is welcome!*
> *Brid is come—Brid is welcome!*

The High Priest lays his staff on the altar.

The ritual continues and neither the High Priest's staff or phallic staff is used again until the later part of the Imbolc Ritual, which is as follows:

The High Priest steps to the side of the altar and three women portraying the triple aspects of the Goddess—the Maiden, the Mother and the Crone—fetch the biddy, the phallic staff, and the candles (now extinguished), from the center of the circle and lay them beside the altar.[11] The ceremony is eventually brought to a close.

The above ritual is one of the few examples where a traditional Wiccan ceremony uses two symbolic staffs. It demonstrates the important symbolism and versatility of the ritual staff in various religious practices.

Previously, in Drawing Down the Moon, the High Priestess is the one who uses the staff. In the Imbolc Ritual, the High Priest uses two staffs when taking the role of the God. Solitary practitioners often take the role of both deities, regardless if it is God or Goddess. As indicated in the Imbolc Ritual, a solitary practitioner could certainly use more than one ritual staff.

Raising the Cone of Power

Once you have a need or purpose for magical work, the energy to affect and alter the current situation and bring necessary change must be raised and then directed. There are religious and magical organizations that use the ritual knife, wand, or simply their hands for this purpose. It is reasonable to state, however, that the staff or any ritual tool you create enhances and inspires your magical work by adding much to your visualization and effectiveness.

Power resides within our bodies; each of us has this power that can be used to "see" in divination (such as reading tarot cards), and in the healing of the sick. Certain individuals can see this power in the form of an aura.

In a coven of witches, the work of magic develops as this power is drawn from each coven member within the consecrated circle and blends harmoniously to form one massive field of energy. This energy, with conformity of one's Will, can cause change to occur in any situation. Obviously, the Will of each coven member must be directed toward the same goal. This power is raised by the combination of visualization, chanting, and dance. Once the power is raised, it collects in the form of a cone over the circle, whether conducted by a group of people or a solitary practitioner. The sufficient power produced must then be directed. Energy without direction is useless and dissipates without result.

There are several formulas for raising energy to produce the Cone of Power. First, decide exactly what type of magical work you wish to conduct. Magic should only be practiced in an area where you will not be disturbed. You must be able to focus all of your energy and concentration into the work you wish to conduct. Take the telephone off the hook, draw the curtains, and make preparations beforehand to have the utmost privacy during your ritual.

You may choose to dress in ritual garb, street clothing, or be naked (formally termed "skyclad" in the Wiccan religion). There is no dress code in magic.

To begin, rest your ritual staff upon the altar. Sacred space preparation, circle casting, calling the elements, and so forth, are the first steps toward readying both your mind and the physical plane for the concentration of energy needed to produce change.

There are many ways to build the power within you—the methods commonly used in the Craft are chanting and dancing. This technique has been employed for thousands of years, and is still utilized by primitive societies today.

Shamanism and Native American rituals employ the use of rhythmic drumming. This can be a simple beat produced by one person for self-preparation, or it can be orchestrated by a group of people using various drums playing a similar beat. The pace of the drumming should be slow at first and progress to a fast beat which builds the energy. Drumming produces physical effects, like raising the pulse, which will assist your efforts.

If you do not have a drum, dancing clockwise around the circle and chanting can set your blood pumping and your energy quickening. The chanting should be rhythmic and the dancing slow at first, then progressively faster. Your heart beat will accelerate, you'll feel hotter, and you will become emotionally excited as the power builds. There will be a climax—you will feel it—and when it arrives, you will know the power has been sufficiently built.

What you chant is your decision; it will surely relate to your spiritual or magical path. Chants do not necessarily have to rhyme or reflect poetry. It is important that the chant be simple and rhythmic, like the following:

> *Clockwise the circle, round and round, power building— magic abound!*

As you build power through energy-raising, focus your mind upon the work to be done. The strongest element in magical work is feeling—you must feel extremely true and strong about what you are trying to accomplish. The changes you desire need to be clearly outlined so that your mind can fully concentrate upon them. Allow the desire for change to engulf you entirely.

As your power is building, focus upon seeing the desired changes finished. Do not suppose the changes will be made—see them accomplished. For example, if you are practicing healing magic for a loved one, you would not concentrate just on the health problem, you would actually visualize the ailment already healed and your loved one healthy. Picture your loved one well again. You do not have to envision the process of healing—see your loved one as having already been healed.

As you complete your dancing, chanting, drumming, and power raising, draw down the power from the Gods to aid your efforts. This is often done if you feel that the power you have raised is not sufficient, or if you are practicing as a solitary.

Your ritual staff assists you in drawing the power down from the Gods. Take your staff in both hands and hold it vertically so it is halfway above your head. Call upon your deities, either silently or aloud, and feel the surge of energy come through the staff and down your arms, to collect in your body.

The power you collect within will feel warm, maybe even hot. Visualization can be an important tool to use when sensing the flowing energies traveling through the ritual staff and into your physical body. Many witches visualize fireworks of color within a circle of bursting divine energy. As the divine energy travels through their body, they may visualize the purest of white light.

At the moment when the drawn power is collected, it is ready to be directed toward your desired purpose. Your body acts as an amplifier during this process.

Stand in the center of your circle with your staff in hand. Grasp the staff's middle with both hands and raise your arms upward to their full extension. The staff's top end now projects the energy above you, forming the Cone of Power as all energy is released at once from your body. It flows within the circle and is amplified through your staff.

Release the power; visualize it shooting through your staff and exiting as a forceful blast of color from the shaft's tip. This process of release is similar in momentum to that of energy unlocked from a firearm. Try to sense the climactic adrenaline slowly decreasing as you release the energy. You may feel relief or momentary weakness as your body chemistry adjusts to its original state. Once the release has been completed, the power is directed and the energy spent.

The pagan's Cone of Power and the Christian's act of prayer are simply highly charged, powerful thought-forms. The thought-form, or creation of your Will, takes on life and being. Pagan religions, such as Wicca, and Christianity both conduct what many term positive magic, that is, the employing of one's personal power and that of the divine for change. Every phase of positive magic is willed. However, it is used only for positive change, and through the practitioner's devotion to their God(s).

Grounding

After the Cone of Power has been released, grounding is essential. Any excess energy that remains within your physical body can result in an unbalanced body and mind. Your body chemistry may be unable to promptly regain its original balance of energy. When grounding is not conducted, individuals often feel nervous, anxious, and tense.

Standing with your staff in both hands, visualize any excess energy drawn from your physical body flowing through your arms, exiting from your hands, and absorbed by your staff. Only energy that remains from the ritual will be absorbed. Once the excess energy resides within your staff, thump the staff's bottom end onto the ground once. The remaining energy is then grounded as it leaves the staff and penetrates into the earth.

There are other ways to perform grounding, such as stomping your feet on the ground. It is unnecessary to conduct additional exercises that lengthen the ritual and exhaust the practitioner. You really only need to perform one grounding ritual. Eating some food immediately after the ritual will also help you ground.

Throughout your rituals, your staff may be used for a variety of symbolic gestures. The Ink Mountain Coven members thump their staff on the ground three times before and after a ritual to symbolize the beginning and ending of the rite.

If you have a coven, small or large, you may decide to devise a format in which the ritual staff may be used by some or all of the members. One idea is to designate four members to represent the four elements who stand, staff in hand, at the four cardinal points during a ritual. The high priest or priestess directs the course of opening the ritual, and each member calls their designated element. This format will benefit the coven since it allows all members to be involved. Each member directs the element during magical work by standing at their respective cardinal points, holding the top ends of their staffs toward the middle of the circle, and projecting the elemental energy toward the priest or priestess conducting the magic work at the circle's center.

A dear friend of ours, who practices an ancient Egyptian religious-magical tradition, uses his ritual staff to greet his God, Ra, symbolized by the Sun. Some may call this a salute, while others consider it calling down the Sun, or calling up the Sun. He simply calls it, "a short ritual I perform three times a day in honor of my Lord, Ra."

The first ritual is performed at dawn, before anything else is done to start the day. He takes his staff (which he calls his "scepter"), and walks out on his backyard deck. He pounds the staff on the deck three times. Then with his right hand he holds the staff high into the air toward the Sun. As he does so, he recites the following sacred words found in the Papyrus of Ani from The Book of the Dead:

> Ra delivers up His two eyes; the Sun and the Moon.
> (Speaking as Ra) I am Khepera in the morning, I am Ra at noon, and I am Tum at even.

With this said, he pounds the scepter three times and the ritual is ended. This rite is repeated in the afternoon and evening.

This gentleman also has a crook, which is a staff with a hooked end, such as that carried by shepherds. He uses the crook during certain other rituals. This is a good illustration of how certain religious or magical paths may use more than one staff.

We offer these examples as food for thought. You may wish to use some of the rituals and applications we have mentioned here to begin to incorporate your ritual staff into your own magical-religious regimen. We are certain that in time you will discover many more uses for your staff in your spiritual work.

Endnotes

1. Diane Stein, *Casting The Circle*, (Freedom, CA: The Crossing Press, 1990), 50.
2. Raymond Buckland, *Buckland's Complete Book of Witchcraft*, (St. Paul: Llewellyn Publications, 1990), 43.
3. Ibid., 43.
4. Stein, *Casting the Circle*, 50.
5. Ibid.
6. Ibid.
7. Taken from the *Ink Mountain Coven Book of Shadows*.
8. Stein, *Casting the Circle*, 53.
9. Janet and Stewart Farrar, *A Witches Bible Compleat*, (New York: Magickal Childe Publishing, Inc., 1981, 1984), 69.
10. Ibid., 70.
11. Ibid., 70-71.

4

Wand Construction and Use

The wand is similar in function to the ritual staff. However, it is much shorter in length and often smaller in diameter. Also, it cannot be used as a walking stick like its larger relative.

The ritual wand has enjoyed continuous usage from ancient times to today. There is plentiful evidence that the wand, like the staff, has been an important attribute of ancient rites. Interesting evidence of this is in linguistic research that shows the symbols cel (of the Celts), or ger (of the Germans), both mean "wand."[1] We find that the Celts and Teutons were wand bearers—they used the wand as the symbol of the axis of the solstices.[2]

Many people are familiar with the fact that the wand was held by and symbolic of kings and dignitaries. It was defined by the ancients as also representing the highest of spiritual maturity. A wand signifies the wisdom of a person who is connected through the power of his or her spirit with the eternal spirit and who thinks and acts accordingly.[2] To Wiccans, the wand represents the element of air.

In contemporary religious and magical practices, the wand has maintained its place as a primary ritual tool with its main function as a tool of invocation. In ritual, the wand is usually held high while words of power are spoken to invoke specific deities to witness the ceremony. It can be used to direct energy, to draw magical symbols, or even to stir brew in the cauldron.[3] The tip of the wand is pointed toward the ground to outline the ritual circle and it is also used to invoke the four elements. The wand's tip usually has some kind of precious stone, such as a quartz crystal or amethyst, to assist in directing energies.

Some people prefer the wand over the ritual staff. Its smaller size makes it more manageable. It can be placed upon the altar when not in use, and is often placed with other ritual tools for storage (unlike the ritual staff, which is often too large and must be stored separately). At certain times, we have made wands for individuals who lived in small studio apartments, shared their living quarters, or who otherwise had limited space in which to conduct rituals. In these instances a ritual staff would be too large, or too noticeable, to use.

The typical wand is shorter and thinner than the staff. Many books state that the wand should measure from your elbow to the tip of your middle finger—or somewhere between fifteen and twenty-one inches. The suggested size for the wand differs from tradition to tradition, so we recommend choosing a length that is most comfortable for you.

The wand is traditionally stored wrapped in a linen cloth or other fabric which has protective, purifying qualities. It is then placed with other ritual implements within an altar, a dresser drawer, or a storage box.

Wands can be made from just about any material and still be durable and manageable. Gorgeous ready-made wands constructed of copper, ivory, and glass are commercially available. These tools are easily managed in ritual, although the glass wands do require special care since they are easily broken.

Wands can also be crafted from copper tubing purchased at hardware stores. A quartz crystal can be inserted and glued into the top end of the tubing and leather or fabric can be wrapped around the entire length of the wand and secured with leather strapping or copper wire. Copper wands are durable, attractive, and effective. Some pagan groups and magical orders consider copper an excellent energy conductor for raising and directing energy.

A Wiccan friend of ours once gave us a copper wand. We had never before used a wand made of copper, and were completely enchanted by it. Although we have devoted most of our practice to tools made of wood, we have fallen in love with this unusual and beautiful wand and have used it successfully many times in our magical work.

Wood remains the favorite material for making wands. It provides the sacred, durable, and attractive look sought by most contemporary pagans for their ritual wands. Hardwoods are most suitable for making wands, and are easier to craft than softwoods like pine.

Certain pagan text books state that "traditional wood"—such as willow, elder, oak, rowan, and apple—must be used to make wands. Celtic religions in particular call for rowan wood, which is extremely difficult to come by since the rowan tree is not common in most of North America. If your religious tradition insists upon using a certain wood type that is simply unavailable to you, choose another tree that is in the same tree family. In human families, the blood line connects the genes and DNA; the same is true for the genetic properties of tree families. The American mountain ash, European mountain ash, and showy mountain ash are all in the same tree family as the rowan tree, are commonly found in many states across America, and are much easier to obtain. Regardless of the wood type, the magical properties and sacred uses of different woods are identical if within the same tree family.

The Basic Ritual Wand

Materials Needed

To make your ritual wand you will need the following tools and materials:

- A branch or commercial wood stock in the length, and thickness that you require
- Sand paper (coarse, medium, and fine grit)
- Vise (optional)
- Wood plane or rasp (optional)
- Wood file (optional)

Step 1   *Determine the size of your wood.*

The instructions for crafting a wand from wood are nearly identical to those given for the ritual staff, except that the wand is much shorter and narrower. Because the wand is smaller than the staff it can be made from a single branch or piece of wood. (In other words, you do not have to glue two identical pieces of wood together to arrive at a desired thickness—one piece of wood should be thick enough.)

You will need to determine the size of the wand suitable for you. Most wands we have crafted for individuals are between fifteen and twenty-one inches in length. The diameter of the wand should be no less than half an inch. If you plan to add a lot of decoration to your wand, you may wish to make it thick enough in diameter to support the added weight. Allow your creativity to take charge!

Step 2   *Obtain your wood.*

Using round stock: Hardware stores, home centers, and lumber yards carry wooden dowels that work remarkably well as wands. Dowels are already rounded to a smooth finish and come in various lengths and diameters. You may purchase a dowel and simply decorate it with symbols and ornaments, simplifying the entire woodworking process. We have seen attractive, beautifully decorated wands made from dowels, and owners of these wands proudly state that their wands serve them well in ritual.

Using square stock: One small piece of wood can be purchased for the wand. Simply use a wood plane, rasp, or file to remove excess wood until you achieve the desired shape for the wand.

Using naturally acquired wood: You can look to nature for a small branch from your chosen tree type. Refer to the instructions listed in chapter 3 on "Acquiring Natural Wood" (page 33). Naturally acquired wood for the wand will require the same drying and bark-removal procedures that were described for the ritual staff.

Step 3   *Shaping.*

Decide how you would like your ritual wand to be shaped. If you have a square piece of commercial wood and want it to be somewhat rounded, follow the same instructions that were given for rounding the ritual staff. Use a wood plane, rasp, or file for shaping the wand.

Step 4   *Determine if sanding is required.*

Sanding is recommended if you would like to stain, finish, or enamel your wand. However, you don't have to sand if you want your wand to have natural irregularities. The choice is yours.

Step 5   *Sanding your wand.*

Sanding should be done from top to bottom and with the grain. Begin with 60 to 80 grit sandpaper. Then proceed to 100 grit. Finally, apply 150 grit sandpaper.

Step 6   *Finishing touches.*

The final step is the application of symbolism and decoration. You can carve, paint, or wood brand your wand. (see chapter 8, "Carving, Painting, and Wood Branding.") You may also decide to glue decorations, such as crystals, leather, fabric, beads, or gemstones, onto your wand.

You may want a wand with the sole purpose of serving you in magic. The wand described below is certain to meet your needs. Although the wand is challenging to make, it is an enjoyable project.

Magician's Wand

Often, the attributes of a Magician's Wand are different from those of a ritual wand. One group of ceremonial magicians, known as the Golden Dawn, uses a specialized wand called a Fire Wand used to represent the element of fire. This wand is constructed of wood and has a long hole drilled through its entire length into which a magnetized wire is inserted. It is thought that the magnetic wire assists the magician in conducting and directing energy.

Although you can make a similar wand yourself, it is not always easy. One simple and traditional solution to this problem is to make the wand from bamboo, which is naturally hollow.

The Magician's Wand described here is similar, though not identical, to the Fire Wand of the Golden Dawn. This is a phallic-shaped wand with a magnetic wire inserted into its interior and extending its entire length. Unlike a Fire Wand, which is always painted with specific colors and symbolism, the Magician's Wand may be decorated in any number of different ways that are personally appealing to its owner.

Materials Needed

Crafting the Magician's Wand requires the following tools and materials:

- Commercial wood stock that is 2" in width, 2" in thickness, and in the length that you require for your wand

- Steel wire that matches the length of your wood and is approximately ⅟₁₆" in diameter

- A small magnet

- An electric drill and a very long drill bit

- Sand paper (coarse, medium, and fine grit)

- Vise

- Wood plane or rasp (optional)

- Wood file (optional)

Step 1   *Determine the size of your wood.*

The length of your wand should be whatever is most comfortable for you. Because the center of the wand will need to be drilled out and the tip of the wand will need to be shaped into a phallic or cone-shape, the Magician's Wand will need to be at least 2" thick.

Step 2   *Obtain your wood.*

If you choose a dowel for your wand, it should be of a 2" diameter. If you prefer square stock, buy a piece that is 2" in width and 2" in thickness. In fact, square stock may be preferable for this project since it is easier to secure a square piece of wood in a vise. (Once the wood has been drilled, you can remove excess wood and round your wand with a wood plane or rasp.)

Step 3   *Obtaining magnetized wire.*

Single pieces of steel wire, 36" in length, can be purchased at hobby stores. If you cannot find any short lengths of wire for sale, use the wire from a straightened clothes hanger.

Note: Copper wire will not work. You must use steel wire or else the magnetic charge will not take.

The wire may need to be cut to match the proper length of your wand, or a little shorter, since the hole drilled will stop about ½" before the end of the wand. The wire should not extend out from the tip of the wand.[4]

The easiest way to obtain magnetic wire is to make it yourself. Simply set the length of wire on a magnetic source, such as a large circular magnet on the back of a refrigerator decoration, for a day or two. Another way to do this is to take the wire and repeatedly move a strong magnet across it in one direction only.

You can test the wire's magnetization by placing it next to another magnet and seeing if there is a reaction, or by seeing if it picks up a small metal object such as a pin or paper clip.

Note: These procedures usually work, but there is always a chance the magnetic field could decrease in time. We suggest obtaining a small magnet, perhaps off the back of a refrigerator decoration, cutting it into tiny pieces, and slipping these pieces into the wand shaft when you insert the wire.

Step 4 *Drilling your wood.*

Note: Use common sense and safety precautions when working with power tools or else you will suffer injury. Eye protection gear is also recommended. A vise attached to a sturdy workbench is essential to this project. See the instructions given in chapter 2 on the proper way of using a drill.

To drill a hole in your wand, you will need an electric drill and a drill bit that is approximately the same width as your wire, or slightly larger. A ³⁄₃₂" or ⅛" bit should do the trick. Get the longest drill bit you can find. You must clamp the wand securely in a work table or vise to ensure it does not slip during drilling.

Drill a hole in the center of the wood and continue until you have drilled a long cavity most of the way through the length of the wand. You will need to drill the cavity nearly through the wand's length, but not out the other end. The hole must be perfectly straight and centered so as not to penetrate the wand's sides. It is not important if you are unable to find a drill bit that will make a cavity through the entire length of your wand. Find the longest possible.

Drilling a long, straight, centered cavity into the wand is not an easy task. If you lack the confidence to drill your own wand, refer to the section entitled "An Alternative to Drilling the Magician's Wand" on page 81.

Step 4. Secure your wood block in a vise and drill a hole down through the center. It does not have to go all the way through the length of your wand.

Step 5 *Shaping*.

If you have used a piece of square stock instead of a round dowel, decide how you would like your wand to be shaped. The top of the wand will need to be crafted into a cone-shape. Draw the shape you desire onto all four sides of the wood with a pencil; this will serve to guide you as you begin to remove the excess wood. Make sure that each of the drawings are centered on all four sides of the wood so that you won't end up with a lop-sided wand. [diagram 5(a)].

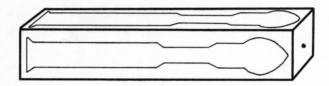

Step 5(a). Draw the outline of the shape you desire for your wand. Be sure to draw it on all four sides of the wood to serve as an accurate guide.

Use a wood plane, rasp, or file for shaping the wand. Turn the wand as you work to insure that the wand will be straight, not crooked. [diagrams 5(b) and 5(c)].

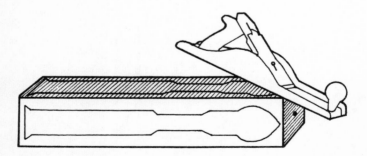

Step 5(b). Use a plane, rasp, or file for shaping your wand. Shown above, a wood plane.

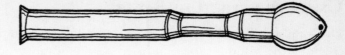

Step 5(c). After you've shaped your wand, it should look something like this.

Step 6   *Determine if sanding is required.*
If you would like to sand your wand, follow the same instructions given earlier for sanding the basic ritual wand.

Step 7   *Inserting the wire.*
Make sure that the wire is magnetized before you finish the wand. Push the wire into the cavity that you created in the center of the wand. Cut off any excess wire. If you choose to insert bits of magnet into your wand, add them at this point.

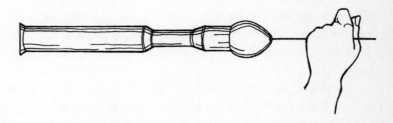

Step 7. Push the magnetized wire into the cavity you have created in the center of the wood.

Step 8   *Finishing touches.*
Add whatever symbolism and decoration you feel is appropriate for your spiritual path. (see chapter 8, "Carving, Painting, and Wood Branding.")

An Alternative to Drilling the Magician's Wand

To create a groove in the Magician's Wand for the insertion of the magnetized wire, you may also use the same methods given for making the groove in the Shaman's Rattle Staff, (Chapter 3). Simply insert the wire into the groove before gluing the two wood pieces together.

Using the Wand in Ritual

The wand is primarily used in the act of invocation. In the Wiccan religion, the wand is not only used for invocation, but also for directing power, projecting and directing raised energy, and in magical work. The wand may also represent the element of air in certain rituals.

The following is a simple invocation of the Goddess which demonstrates how the wand may be used. This invocation has been altered slightly to make it fairly generic—so that readers from any spiritual tradition may use it as an exercise for becoming accustomed to working with a wand.

The casting of a circle is performed as usual (see chapter 3). The wand can be used as a substitute for the ritual staff in this rite. Hold the wand's shaft with one or both hands and point its top end toward the ground. Follow this procedure with the purification process that your spiritual path employs, such as the sprinkling of holy water or salt water around the circle, or waving the incense around the circumference of your ritual area. Then, using the wand, call the four elements according to your particular tradition, or as outlined on the ritual staff.

Remember, there are only two real differences between the ritual staff and wand. The wand is smaller and primarily used for invocation. Therefore, it is possible to use both implements in the same ritual or interchangeably. The following pages illustrate examples of how the wand can be used in ritual.

Drawing Down the Moon

This invocation of the Goddess, described in Chapter 3, is performed for reverence and to absorb the Goddess' power. It is often done with the ritual staff, but can also be done just as effectively with the wand.

To perform this rite with your wand, stand in the center of the circle with the wand raised in both hands with its point toward the heavens. Speak words of invocation such as:

(Goddess name of your choice) *of the Moon, thou Great*
Mother to all creatures that dwell upon this Earth. I call upon
you this night to fill me with the joy of spiritual maturity,
instruct me in the wisdom of fulfillment, and bathe me with
your divine presence. Grant that I shall honor thee this night.

There is no need to move the wand at all during the invocation.
Its top end is pointed high above you—absorbing the energies and
presence of the Goddess as she descends into your temple or circle.
The wand, in this case, acts as a channel of sorts; guiding the power
and presence of the Goddess through the wand tip, down your arms,
and into your body.

Handfasting

The Wiccan handfasting rite exhibits the wand's role in a ritual well.
Handfasting is the Wiccan marriage ritual. The ceremony unites a
man and woman "for as long as love shall last."

The wand is used exclusively in many Wiccan traditions for the rite
of handfasting. A particular wand is used—the Priapic Wand—named
after the Roman God Priapus who symbolized procreation and is
similar to the Wiccan God Pan, the Greek nature deity. The Priapic
Wand is the phallic symbol of the God and typically measures
between eighteen and twenty-one inches. Nine inches of the bottom
end is wider than the wand's overall shaft, and it is carved to look like
the male organ. You could attach a pine cone to the top of the Priapic Wand, or carve the wand's tip to look like a stalk of grain. This
wand is not typically incorporated into ritual practice except for special rites such as handfasting.

Male witches often use the Priapic Wand, or one similar, to represent the God in their work. This is not to suggest that women should
shy away from its use; female witches often construct a phallic wand
to help them become more attuned to their Lord in ritual.

The handfasting rite is performed on either the waxing or the full
moon. The altar is decorated with blossoming flowers. Rose buds are
tossed around the circle and a sweet, romantic incense, such as jas-
mine or rose, is lit for the occasion. The usual ritual preparation is as
follows: ritual bathing is performed, ritual tools and ceremonial decorations are arranged upon the altar, and salt and water are mixed

together to use for the purification of the circle. When the rite begins, the circle is cast, the elements are called, and then the deities are invoked.

The handfasting rite outlined below demonstrates how a coven may perform the ceremony using a wand. Legally ordained Wiccan ministers (priests and priestesses) can perform a handfasting for all Wiccans who desire a marriage ceremony.

Once the opening steps of the ritual have taken place, the coven members station themselves at the circle's boundary; the High Priest and Priestess stand directly before the altar with the bride and groom at the center of the circle facing them.

The Priest and Priestess exchange a kiss that symbolizes the love and union of the marrying couple.

An appointed coven member announces the bride and groom thus:

> *The couple in our midst seek the bond of handfasting and union of their blossoming love.*

The Priestess replies:

> *May they be named and brought forth.*

The coven member states:

> (groom's name) *is the man whom seeks* (bride's name).
> (bride's name) *is the woman who seeks* (groom's name).

The bride and groom step forward to stand before the Priest, Priestess, and the altar. The bride usually stands opposite the Priest and the groom is across from the Priestess.

The Priestess asks the groom if the name stated is indeed his true name. She then asks him what he desires. He answers:

> *To unite with* (bride's name), *in the eyes of my Lord and Lady.*

The Priest makes the same inquiries of the bride.

Thereafter, the Priestess takes up the ritual dagger (see chapter 5) and raises it high into the air. The Priest takes the Priapic Wand from the altar and hands it to the bride and groom, who hold it by the ends between them with both hands. The wand symbolizes the union between the couple in marriage, and represents procreation in hopes that the union may be a fruitful and fertile one.

The Priestess announces

> *Lord and Lady, witness before you two of your people who*
> *declare their love seeking your blessing for marriage.*

Marriage vows are exchanged. The Priapic Wand is held firmly with the hopes, sincerity, and love between the bride and groom. After the vows are concluded, the exchange of rings follows. The bride and groom then hold the Priapic Wand in their left hands and cup their right hands to receive their rings. Blessings and words of wisdom meant to encourage the marriage are spoken by both the Priest and Priestess.

The ceremony closes with a harmonious, "So Mote It Be!" by all individuals present. The Priest takes the Priapic Wand from the couple. The bride and groom exchange rings. The two exchange a kiss, and then exchange kisses with the Priest and Priestess. The bride and groom walk the circle's circumference and are congratu-lated by all attending. Finally, the ritualistic Cakes and Ale Cere-mony is performed.

The Priapic Wand plays a significant role in the handfasting cere-mony. It represents the positive goals of marriage, and the couple's unconditional, loving union. The wand is usually decorated with a flowing, colorful ribbon, and anointed with essential oil that has been blessed.

In some Wiccan traditions, such as the Gardnerian tradition, a symbolic ribbon or cord is tied around the bride and groom's hands as they each take hold of the Priapic Wand.

Evocation

Some pagan religions and other magical groups use a phallic-shaped wand for a variety of ritual purposes; the Golden Dawn's Fire Wand is used to invoke or banish the element of fire in magical workings.

The Magician's Wand described earlier is used in magical work to assist in building, directing, and projecting energies, and coupled with the magician's will, to succeed at achieving the desired change. It is often employed for the evocation of entities, which are conjured to be of service to the magician—to carry out tasks in order for the magical work to succeed. The process of evocation can be potentially dangerous and requires years of proper training. Not every entity is thrilled to be conjured by a magician who draws upon its power and manipulates that power for his own reasons. The magician must be skilled and mentally balanced, and his reasons for performing the evocation must be just and sincere.

The magician absorbs an entity's power, or any other source of energy, through the wand, which acts as a channel to enhance the magical work. The magician may, at times, extend his or her own energies or "power" through the wand. This power exits through the tip and is directed as needed.

The wand is used differently in the techniques of invocation and evocation. Through invocation, the practitioner is extracting the power and presence of a deity through sacred words recited in preparation of ritual work. Thus the power of the deity is invoked into the practitioner. Deities are not commanded or manipulated through invocation. Through evocation, the practitioner summons forth an entity, spirit, or elemental being into visible appearance for the sake of achieving a specific magical goal.

There is a great satisfaction and enjoyment in creating your own wand and using it in your spiritual and magical practice. Your wand should be as unique as you are. Having been created by your hands, we know it will serve you well.

Endnotes

1. Marie-Lu Lorler, *Shamanic Healing* (Albuquerque: Brotherhood of Life, 1989), 37-38.
2. Ibid., 38.
3. Scott Cunningham, *Wicca: A Guide For The Solitary Practitioner*, (St. Paul: Llewellyn Publications, 1990), 27.
4. A Golden Dawn style Fire Wand has the magnetized wire sticking approximately $\frac{1}{16}$" out of both ends of the wand.

5

Ritual Knife Construction and Use

Any knife that suits you can function as a ritual knife. Hunting and weaponry shops offer an assortment of futuristic, medieval, and gothic styles, and a variety of shapes, sizes, and blades. However, you can extract a purer sense of self, spiritualism, and magical results through the personal construction and use of a ritual dagger.

The origin of the use of daggers in pagan rituals is uncertain and the subject of much disagreement among pagan scholars. It is clear, however, that numerous magical and religious traditions, ancient and modern, used a knife of some kind in ritual.

The ritual knife, dagger, or athame, represents a subtle energy not easily comprehended by an individual who has never used the tool in spiritual or magical practice. Many people think of the knife as a weapon of destruction, combat, and victory. These common descriptions offer clues to the knife's ritualistic role; destruction of evil, combat in life (survival), and victory within the natural and unnatural worlds. The ancient use of the knife constituted a force or power that was easily understood and recognized. Often, the ancient rites recognized the ritual dagger as the magician's power manifested in matter.

In contemporary paganism, the ritual knife is not usually used for cutting. Different pagan traditions use the ritual knife for different reasons and roles. Often it is incorporated into ritual for the casting or closing of the circle and is frequently associated with the masculine aspects of Nature—the God. The phallic structure of the ritual knife links it to the Wiccan God. One use descended from ancient practice still exists—the tool channels and tames the imperceptible energies of the religious or magical cause (the will of the owner), and enables them to be used in ritual.

In Wicca, the ritual knife is primarily used to direct energy raised during spells and ritual and to channel energy through the knife. The athame is a tool that causes change, and it is an instrument of power, manipulation, and command.

Members of the Golden Dawn use an Air Dagger, a double-edged blade with a "T" shaped wooden handle. It represents the element of Air and is restricted from cutting any living thing.

Essentially, your ritual knife may be used for whatever purpose you deem fit under the ethical and constructive practices of your path.

This honored tool is considered extremely personal. Many pagan traditions stress this personal nature by not using another practitioner's knife. In some cases of working partners, a couple, or a coven, this etiquette is bypassed by acquiring the owner's permission. Unlike other pagan paths, witchcraft considers the athame a personal tool belonging to one witch only, not shared even within a coven. This demonstrates how the role of the ritual knife differs symbolically from that of the other ritual tools mentioned in this book.

The design of your personal knife is entirely a matter of choice. The knife blade is usually made of steel, although many functioning and attractive knives have been crafted of bronze, copper, and flint blades. The knife handle can be fashioned from wood, stone, horn, deer's foot, or an assortment of materials. In this chapter we will focus on constructing a ritual dagger with a wood handle and a steel blade; this choice results in a finished tool that is small, light, and easily manageable within sacred practices.

The ritual knife is on of the most difficult of the projects discussed in this book, and requires a thorough reading of the various construction techniques used for crafting the other tools. It would be better for a beginner to work through other projects first to gain some experience and skill. Otherwise, you may end up starting the knife project over several times because of mistakes. People often have a sophisticated, intricate design in mind, and they become frustrated when trying to create these complex designs. The instructions we supply here are simple, effective, and can be modified to suit your crafting needs should you desire a knife handle of more detailed design. Notice that we are specifically discussing crafting the handle; unless you are a blacksmith or machinist and can make your own knife blade with precision, it is best to purchase a knife blade. There may be a local knife shop in your area that sells blades. For information on commercial sources that sell knife blades, see the Resources Guide on page 213.

Be aware that some knife blades, although of excellent quality, have screw threads at the handle end (tang) that are metric, probably because they are made overseas. Unfortunately these blades do not arrive with fasteners, usually called nuts. Finding nuts in the United States to use with them is tricky. You can take the blade to a hardware store so that the attendant there can match the threads up to a correct nut. If this doesn't work, try an auto parts store. They may have nuts you can use. You may also try a pommel to screw onto the screw threads. It is best to obtain professional advice on this matter from a hardware store or home center.

The size of your knife should be to your comfort and liking. Knife blades come in many sizes. A completed ritual knife that measures eight inches in entire length is a nice size for ritual work.

Since the blade comes with a tang (handle part of the blade) that penetrates the wooden knife handle you will craft, you can make a longer wooden handle for decorative purposes if so desired. However, if your blade has screw threads at the tang end you will be unable to make a longer handle because a bolt must be placed at the tang end, which prohibits a handle longer than the size of your tang. Before you order the blade, get precise measurements to make sure it is what you had in mind for size.

The Basic Ritual Knife

Materials Needed

To make your ritual knife you will need
the following tools and materials:

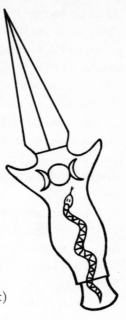

- Wood (natural or commercial) in
  the length and thickness that you
  require.

- A knife blade

- A nut or pommel that fits the screw
  threads of the knife's tang

- Vise

- C-clamps

- Wood plane or rasp or wood file

- Elmer's Wood Glue

- Sand paper (coarse, medium, and fine grit)

There are two basic methods used to craft a wooden handle for a ritual knife, both of which are tricky. The first, described next, involves
using two separate pieces of wood.

Making a Knife Handle from Two Pieces of Wood

Step 1   *Determine the size of the wood needed.*

First, measure the length of the handle shaft (tang) of the blade. Cut or obtain two pieces of wood that are at least long enough to cover the tang (these can be as long as you wish, if the tang does not have screw threads. If it has screw threads, the length of the wood should be the same as the distance between the base of the blade and the beginning of the screw threads). The wood should be at least one inch thick and one inch wider than the widest part of the tang—you can always shape the handle once secured onto the blade tang.

Step 2   *Tracing the outline of the tang.*

Lay the tang centered onto each piece of wood. Draw around it. If your blade has screw tangs, be sure that they extend from the rear of the wood blocks.

Step 2(a). Trace the tang of your knife blade onto the wood.

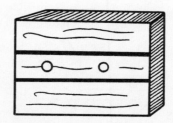

Step 2(b). The outline of the blade tang will be your guide for hollowing out the wood block.

Step 3   *Removing wood for the placement of the tang.*

Use a chisel or carving tool to dig out the inside of the outlined sections, and be careful not to chisel too deeply or outside of the outline. Once you've dug out the groove, lay the
tang onto one piece of wood and lay the other on top. Do
both pieces of wood fit around the tang securely and evenly?
Is one piece of wood chiseled out too much? Not enough?
Slowly make adjustments. Now, if the pieces of wood are
slightly misaligned, that is okay. They can be glued together
and reshaped with a wood plane or file later.

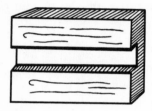

Step 3. Remove the wood from inside your tracing marks with a
chisel. Be sure not to dig too deeply.

Step 4   *Gluing the wood.*

Take the two pieces of wood and slightly roughen the area
on the same side as the outlines. You can do this by nicking
the wood surface with a sharp object all around the outline
area. Then spread either Elmer's Wood Glue or an epoxy
resin glue generously over the entire surface of each wood
piece. Apply glue in the groove where the tang rests, as well.
[diagram 4(a)].

Step 4(a). Apply wood glue or epoxy resin generously to both
pieces of wood.

Place the two pieces of wood together, with the tang of the knife between them. Remember to leave the knife's blade screw threads visible and outside the wooden end of your handle (In a later step, you will need to place the nut upon the screw threads after drying to secure the knife blade so that it will not slide out of the handle). [diagram 4(b)]

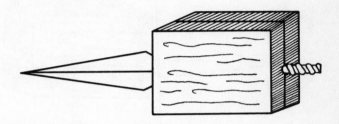

Step 4(b). Place the pieces of wood together with the blade tang between, resting in the groove. Press together tightly.

Step 5 *Clamping.*

Once you've applied the glue, use a vise or C-clamp to tightly hold the two pieces together. The wooden handle must be allowed to dry thoroughly in place for three to five days. If you use a vise to secure the wood for gluing be sure to point the blade of the knife facing away from you.

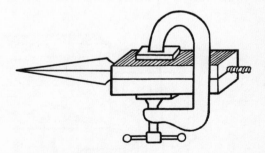

Step 5. Securely clamp the knife and allow to dry 3 to 5 days.

Step 6   *Drawing your design on the handle.*
Before attempting to shape the handle, use a ruler and pencil to carefully measure an outline to cut or file around. This way you know exactly how much of the wood piece needs to be removed.

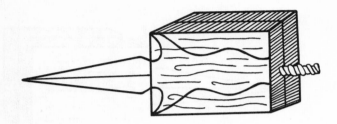

Step 6. Draw the desired shape of your knife handle on the wood blocks.

Step 7   *Securing the knife for shaping.*
Before attempting to shape the handle, cover the blade completely by wrapping it several times a sturdy fabric such as canvas. Then secure the blade into a vise on your work table to prevent the knife from slipping and causing injury while you shape the handle. Make certain that the knife is securely fastened in the vise, with the blade pointed away from you, before you begin work on the handle.

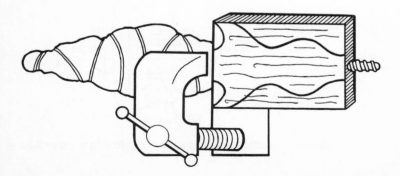

Step 7. Secure the knife in a vise and wrap the blade before beginning to shape your handle.

Step 8   *Shaping your handle.*

You may be able to use a small saw, such as a coping saw, to cut away the wood in the shape indicated in the diagram, or you could use a wood file or plane to slowly shape the wooden handle accordingly. (This step is similar to carving.) Take your time and work a little of the wood away at a time. Once the points on the design are established, you only have to shape the handle in any other manner you desire, and file the handle to a circular or squared-off shape.

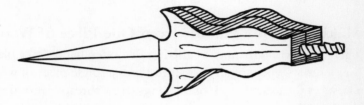

Step 8. Shape your handle with a small saw, wood file, or plane following the guides penciled on the wood.

Step 9   *Covering the screw threads of the tang.*

If you selected a knife blade with screw threads at the end of the tang, screw a nut or pommel over the end of the exposed screw threads. If you don't like the appearance of the nut or pommel projecting from the back end of your ritual knife, hardware and lumber stores sell wooden caps that you can fit over the bolt or pommel and glue into place.

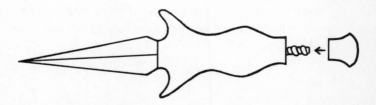

Step 9. Cover the screw threads of the protruding tang with a nut or pommel.

Step 10 *Finishing touches.*

Sand the handle to a smooth finish if you like. From there you can paint the handle entirely, or stain it if you wish. Afterwards, you can apply your symbols and decorations.

The last step, after paint, stain, and application of your symbols, is to spray or brush on a thin layer of protective clear coat or sealant, such as varnish. Your handling of the knife could, in time, wear away the paint on the handle. Stain does not require the application of varnish since it actually penetrates the wood pores.

Making a Knife Handle from One Piece of Wood

There is a second manner of affixing a wooden handle to a blade that uses a screw-type tang. This method uses a single piece of wood that measures the exact length of the tang; screw threads must extend out the end of the wooden handle. Excessive width of the wood is not important if you do not mind filing or planing away the extra later.

In addition to the other tools mentioned earlier in this chapter, you will also need an electric drill and a drill bit.

Step 1 *Securing the wood.*

Once you have obtained your wood in the proper length, the drill, and a bit, you must secure the wood piece firmly in the jaws of a vise that is fastened to a workbench.

Step 2 *Measuring and marking.*

With the wood piece securely held vertically in place, take a ruler and pencil to mark the exact center of the end in which you will place the blade. This is an important step since you do not want the wood piece to fit over the tang unevenly, with one side predominating over the other. (diagram 2, page 97)

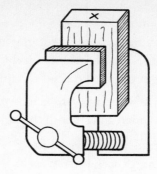

Step 2. Secure your wood block and mark the exact center of the wood.

Step 3 *Drilling the center cavity for the tang.*

Before proceeding, refer to safety tips given in chapter 2 concerning the electric drill.

The length of the drill must be long enough for it to penetrate the entire length of your wood piece and slightly wider than the tang. Drill a hole lengthwise through the wood. This hole should be just large enough so that the tang will pass through it. If the drill bit is too thin, simply shift from side-to-side while drilling, or drill two or more holes on either side of the center hole to enlarge the diameter of the tang cavity.

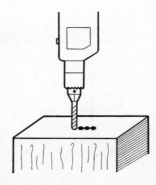

Step 3. Use a hand-held electric drill to bore holes through the center of your wood block.

Keep in mind that this step is tricky. You must hold the drill perfectly centered and straight or the hollow interior for the tang may become crooked, in which case the tang may not fit into the drilled cavity properly. While drilling, evenly apply a little pressure. Proceed carefully and slowly.

Note: A small wood file can be inserted into the new cavity and used to widen and smooth the holes created by the drill.

Step 4   *Fitting the tang into the wood.*

If the drilling process produces an uneven cavity, do not panic. When you finish drilling, try sliding the tang into the cavity. If it fits but is lop-sided, so be it, as long as you have sufficient wood on either side to form a handle. If the tang does not fit properly, you can attempt to re-drill the cavity to widen it. Do this slowly as to not make it too wide. Continue until the tang fits or until it becomes apparent the tang simply will not fit into the wood piece. In such a case, you will have to start the project again.

Step 5   *Covering the screw threads of the tang.*

When the tang is inserted into the wood piece, bolt it in place by screwing a nut to the screw thread end of the tang You now have a wooden handle that looks like a square or rectangular piece of wood. If the tang is loose in the cavity, pour Elmer's Wood Glue into the tang cavity and let it dry thoroughly.

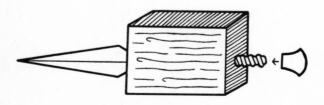

Step 5. When the knife blade is inserted into the handle, cover the screw threads of the tang with a nut.

Step 6 *Shaping the wood.*

The next step is to use a wood file, rasp, or wood plane to shape the handle. The design of the handle may be as simple or sophisticated as you feel your abilities allow.

Step 7 *Finishing touches.*

Sand the handle to a smooth finish if desired. Then you can paint or stain the handle if you wish. Add any symbols and decorations that you feel are appropriate. Finally, apply a coat of sealant to the handle for protection.

Ritual Knife Use

As with the ritual staff, the ritual knife has been used for thousands of years in religious and magical rites and is still used in most contemporary pagan religions and magical orders.

In the Wiccan religion, two knives are used. The first, simply called the magical knife, or athame, is not used for cutting, but to direct energy raised during rituals and spells. Although it is used much like the ritual staff, the magical knife is not a tool for invocation in most cases. It is used to command and manipulate energy. In Wicca, the knife is double-edged with a blade that is usually dull and the handle is a dark color such as brown or black. It is thought that the magical knife, when used in directing energies, will absorb some of those energies into the handle to be used in future magical work. Depending upon the particular Wiccan tradition, some consider the magical knife to be associated with the element of Fire, while others associate it with the element of Air.

The second knife used in Wicca is the White-Handled Knife, also called a *bolline*. It is used for cutting tree branches for wands and staffs, cutting herbs to be used in rites, and carving symbols onto candles and wood. The bolline is considered a practical, working knife, rather than a ritualistic knife. The White-Handled Knife may be used outside of the ritual circle for these purposes.

Some people use the ritual knife for the sole purpose of invocation. It is occasionally used instead of the staff to cast the ritual circle and outline the circle's circumference. The technique of casting a circle is the same, whether one uses the ritual knife or the ritual staff. During the casting of the circle in Wicca, the High Priestess and Priest or the solitary practitioner will take up the athame and draw the Pentagram of Earth over each of the four quarter candles, which represent the elements.

Your own religious tradition or magical order may have specific instructions for using a ritual knife. However, should you be unfamiliar with the ritual knife and how it may benefit your practices, the following example shows how this tool may be used in a Wiccan rite. Wicca is a diversified tradition and the athame (ritual knife) is used in a variety of different ways.

Consecration of the Cakes and Ale

The Wiccan consecration ritual known as "the Consecration of Cakes and Ale," demonstrates the knife's role in a ritual. The Cakes and Ale Ceremony is a ritual ingestion of food and drink that helps the practitioner make the transition back from the ecstasy of the ritual work to normal consciousness. It assists in grounding the residual energies after magical work. This rite is also seen as sacred in itself, since the act of eating is a form of absolute communion and food contains the manifestation of divine energy.

Actually a small meal, the food is blessed before being consumed and a libation dish is partially filled with food and drink as an offering to the God and Goddess. The Cakes and Ale ceremony is a way to give thanks to the Gods for providing the necessities of life including food, and drink. This rite is a link between the ritual work of the Wiccans' meeting, which honors the deities, and the social aspects of being part of a coven.

A ritual knife symbolically represents the male aspect of the God in the consecration of the Cakes and Ale. In a typical solitary witch's practice, a plate of muffins, donuts, bread, or even cookies sits upon the altar. Next to it is a goblet, chalice, or drinking vessel filled with beer, wine, apple juice, milk, or the drink of personal preference. After the completion of the ritual work, the witch stands before the

altar and meditates momentarily, reflecting on the work just performed and paying reverence to the deities. When ready, he or she
proceeds with the Cakes and Ale phase of the ritual by stating:

> *The time has come to give thanks to the Lord and Lady for
> that which sustains our life. I shall ever be aware of all that I
> share with thee.*

The witch grasps the athame with the right hand and takes the vessel
containing the drink into the left hand. Slowly, the practitioner lowers the point of the athame into the drink, symbolically portraying
the union of female (the goblet or drinking vessel) and male (the ritual knife/athame), and states:

> *Life is the fruit of the union between male and female, mak-
> ing possible happiness and prosperity. Throughout all lands
> shall spread fruitfulness and wealth.*

Then the witch lowers the athame, and places it upon the altar. He or
she drinks from the goblet, and replaces the vessel upon the altar.
The athame is again taken up. The witch touches the cakes with the
point of the athame and states:

> *The Gods have blessed this food and I partake of it freely. My
> body partakes of it freely.*

After a brief pause, the reverence continues:

> *Without the Gods I would have naught. I enjoy these gifts of
> the Gods in their honor. So Mote It Be!*

In this ritual, the knife clearly has two different functions. It symbolizes the male polarity and acts as a channel for the witch's consecration of the food and drink.

✦   ✦   ✦

The next two chapters focus on ritual tools that are much more simple in their construction than the staff, wand, and knife—a rune set and a magical or medicine shield. Chapters 8 through 11 focus on ritual tool decoration and techniques. As we conclude this chapter remember that it is not important how sophisticated or well-made your finished ritual tool is. Not everyone is an artist. As long as you are pleased with your completed project, your ritual tool will serve you well in religious and magical work. Your tool is not supposed to look identical to the machine-manufactured, commercial ritual tools in catalogs. Yours is self-created, unique, and will give you the utmost pleasure in its service.

6

Rune Set Construction and Use

Runes are a method of divination from ages past consisting of an alphabet of symbols. Each symbol has a specific divinatory meaning that guides the seeker in a reading or runecast. The word rune comes from a root word meaning "a secret" or "to whisper." It relates to an ancient time when the invention of writing had not yet been established and arcane knowledge was transmitted orally. Runes are also known by the word "mystery," for they represent what can be understood and experienced, but cannot be taught since it cannot be expressed by mere words.

Teutonic races in ancient times created the runes as sacred symbols that served as a system of magic and philosophy. For generations, this system was transmitted by word-of-mouth from shaman to pupil.

Some authors maintain that the runic knowledge died out in the seventeenth century. This is not so. In 1639 C.E., the Christian Church forbade the use of runes, and as a result no one dared to admit using them for fear of persecution. Runic knowledge certainly continued and grew—just as witchcraft survived the persecutions of the Church and various witch hunts. Rune systems were eventually recorded in written language and today its teachings are widely available for interested students.

In this chapter we will discuss the construction of rune staves from wood, including the carving or painting of a rune alphabet onto the staves. We will explore the many runic alphabets available for you to choose from, but we will focus on one in particular—the Elder Futhark. We will explain each rune meaning so that you may use your handmade rune set for divination immediately after its creation.

Runes are commonly engraved upon stones or bones, but wood has long been the preferred material for making runes. Words for "pieces of wood" associated with the runes are numerous.[1] Three Old Norse examples of this are *stafr* (stave, letter, or secret lore), *teinn* (twig, talismanic word for divination), and *hlutr* (lot for divination, talismanic object). The various figures of the runic alphabet are engraved, carved, or painted upon wooden rune staves.

The first step in creating your rune set is to decide the exact number of rune staves you need to make. The number of staves you desire will depend upon the rune alphabet or system you wish to use. There are four different rune alphabets to choose from, and there are various opinions on the exact number of runes for each alphabet.

The Elder Futhark or Germanic system has twenty-four runes, and this is the system that we will detail on the following pages. Other rune alphabets include the Scandinavian rune alphabet, which consists of sixteen runes in either Dutch or Swedish. The Seax-Wica system consists of thirty runes. The Anglo-Saxon alphabet is comprised of three individual systems: the Ruthwell and the Vienna, which both have twenty-eight runes; and the Thames, which has twenty-nine staves. If you choose to use an alphabet other than the Elder Futhark, there are many books available to help you. Refer to the Suggested Reading section for a list of books detailing the history and variations of the different rune systems.

For the purpose of this book, we will concentrate upon the ancient and ever popular Elder Futhark rune alphabet containing twenty-four symbols.

ᚠ ᚢ ᚦ ᚨ ᚲ ᚷ ᚹ ᚺ ᚾ ᛁ ᛃ ᛇ
ᛈ ᛉ ᛊ ᛏ ᛒ ᛗ ᛖ ᛞ ᛚ ᛜ ᛟ

Runic Alphabet. Elder Futhark (24 runes).

Rune Set Construction

Materials Needed

When the time arrives to begin crafting your runes, you will need the following items:

- Branch or dowel
- Small hand saw or sharp, serrated knife (a steak knife will work)
- Sandpaper
- Paints and brushes, small carving tools, or wood branding tools for application of rune symbols

Step 1 *Obtaining your wood.*

When venturing into nature for your rune branch, look for one approximately ½-inch in diameter. The length of the branch should be about 1½ to 2 feet, because you'll want plenty of wood to work with in case a mistake is made. You may even wish to make a second set for a friend. Cutting the branch is easy to do with a knife or garden cutters, though you might find a suitable branch on the ground.

You may wish to consider a tree's magical properties when deciding on the type of wood to use for a rune set (see chapter 1). You should choose a tree that means something to you, whether it conjures up childhood memories, has beautiful foliage, or contains powerful energy. Always remember to ask the tree's permission before taking any wood from it, and thank the tree for its contribution to your project.

If you obtain your rune branch from nature, you will need to allow several days of drying time in case the branch is moist from dew or rain. The bark of the tree branch may be left on or stripped off before cutting. This decision is entirely your own. If you desire smoothly sanded runes, then it will be necessary to remove the bark.

For those of you who live in the city, or do not have the time to go branch hunting, you can visit any lumber or hardware store and purchase an already sanded, well rounded dowel rod from which to make your runes. The wood should measure ½-inch in diameter 1½ to 2 feet in length. Dowels do not offer an extensive selection of wood type, but often come in oak and other popular woods.

It is important to remember that you should be able to hold all of your runes at once in both cupped palms of your hands. Each rune should be no larger than five centimeters long, one centimeter thick and four centimeters wide.

Step 2   *Measuring and cutting.*

With a pencil, measure your wood off into twenty-four staves of roughly equal proportion. [diagram 2(a)]

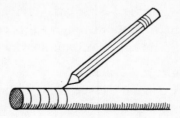

Step 2(a). Measure the width of each rune stave onto your piece of wood and trace them with a pencil.

Secure the wood in a vise or hold it firmly against a workbench as you cut off the individual staves. [diagram 2(b)]. Since you are cutting the branch or dowel as you would slice a cucumber, your runes will be round—these are the easiest runes to make and work with. Rune staves can also be oval, square, rectangular, or any other shape that attracts you.

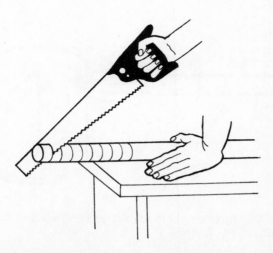

Step 2(b). Saw each stave off of your wood following the measurements you'd traced in step 2(a).

Simply cut the shape you desire from your wood. Odd shaped runes that need more cutting and shaping may require a larger piece of wood for greater manageability.

Step 3 *Sanding.*

After the rune staves are cut, you may wish to use sandpaper to gently smooth rough edges caused by the cutting. This will help ensure comfortable handling.

Step 4 *Applying rune symbols.*

You may choose to carve, paint, or brand the rune symbols onto your staves. Carving is very difficult on such small pieces of wood. An X-ACTO knife, a razor knife which can be purchased at any hardware store, works well for this. Small woodcarving blades for the X-ACTO can be purchased, and are recommended if you choose this method. Keep in mind that unless the wood is stained, the carvings may not show well on the wood surface, making divination difficult. Acrylic paints can be used; they are bright, durable, and easy to clean up. Oil paints are more of a challenge, but can work well. You can also use paint pens or paint markers to apply the symbols as discussed in chapter 8. Red is a traditional color for rune markings on staves.

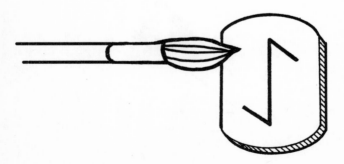

Step 4. Apply one rune to each stave using a paint marker, small brush, or X-ACTO knife.

Step 5 *Staining—optional.*

Stain can be applied before painting or after carving. Some people feel that applying stain as a finish will hinder work with the runes. We do not believe a light application of stain will make a difference.

Varnish, clear protective coats, and shellac should not be applied to the rune staves. Runes are meant to guide, teach, and serve you in magic and divination. Applying a finish to the rune staves seals off the wood pores, blocking valuable energies. Such finishes cover so thickly that you will no longer be able to feel the wood's natural surface with your fingertips.

Runes are often kept in their own pouch for storage and transport. You may purchase one or craft your own.

Rune Divination

Learning rune divination techniques can benefit your magical practice tremendously. Reading a runecast can reveal much hidden knowledge about yourself, your life, and your spiritual path.

The subject of rune divination is extensive and can require much time and careful study. In the following pages, we will describe the basics of divination with runes. The common divinatory meanings of each rune in the Elder Futhark alphabet is briefly listed along with a few simple divination layouts. The information here is by no means comprehensive. This is just the tip of the iceberg, but it will help get you off to a good start.

The following is a basic vocabulary of the important factors in runic divination. Please keep in mind that these are elementary instructions designed to help you familiarize yourself with runes and runic divination.

Reading

This term refers to the procedure of divination from the moment you initially scatter your runes from their pouch to the point at which you have fully determined and examined what the runecast reveals in meaning. "Reading" is this process, whereas the person conducting the reading is called a "reader."

Runecast

The pattern in which the runes are laid out before you actually read them. You may choose an established layout pattern for your runes or simply scatter them and work from there.

Querent or Seeker

The person who is consulting the runes for needed information. You should study and practice rune divination a great deal before attempting a rune reading for someone other than yourself. Be certain you know the rune symbols and definitions well.

Positive and Negative

A positive rune is one that will bring happiness or fulfillment to the seeker in light of the question asked with regard to the seeker's present requirements. A negative rune prevents or withholds the achievement of success or some other positive trait the seeker hopes to attain.

The terms "positive and negative" are not to be considered as meaning good or evil. We all know that sometimes bad news turns out to be the best thing that could happen. In runic philosophy, the trend of evolution is always progressive.

Upright and Reversed

Usually a rune that has both upright and reversed positions is easily recognized. This type of rune usually has two distinct meanings. When the rune is upright it is called positive; when it is reversed it is called negative.

Non-reversible

All runes can be reversed; however it is not always possible to distinguish whether certain runes are upright or reversed because the symbol looks the same either way. An example of this is DAEG.

Position

This term describes where a rune falls in a runecast.

Result or Resultant Position

Some rune definitions include the statement, "this rune means this or that in a result position." Many runecasts include a position which indicates the result or outcome of the question under review.[2] This placement may consist of either one rune or a pair of runes and is usually, though not always, the last rune or pair of runes to be laid out.[3]

Non-reversible runes have a different or expanded meaning when in the result position, and others may have a strengthened meaning or significance when placed there.[4]

Prominent Position

In certain runecasts, some runes are placed in positions that are more important than others. The result position, should there be one, is always of primary interest and concern to the Querent. If the question or problem is not stated directly, you may sense a particular rune that indicates special importance or presents itself as a central symbol. In this case, that rune would be the one you would focus on as central to the reading. Neighboring runes would be read to give an indication of what is on the seeker's mind or what the seeker needs to know in answer to the question.

Allow your intuition to guide you. What does or does not constitute a prominent position can vary from reading to reading, and as you gain experience you will find that any placement can attain the status of a prominent position simply by virtue of the fact that, as you turn over a particular rune, something clicks in your subconscious that tells you: "This is the one. This is the root of the problem."[5]

This section examines each of the Elder Futhark runes and provides thumbnail descriptions of their divination meanings. These descriptions are based two excellent books on the subject: *The Runic Workbook*, by Tony Willis, (Sterling Publishing, 1990), and *A Practical Guide To The Runes*, by Lisa Peschel, (Llewellyn Publications, 1989).

Each description specifies how the rune should be read in either upright or reversed position. All rune illustrations shown on the following pages are in their "upright" positions. "Reversed" runes would be upside-down. Non-reversible runes require an examination of the surrounding runes to help determine the exact reading.

The Elder Futhark Runes

FEHU

Upright: Primary meaning is that of wealth; also it indicates earned income and monetary or material gain. If its neighbors are love runes, it can signify romantic gain. Upright, it indicates the ability to win over opposing forces.

Reversed: This position indicates a loss or disappointment of sorts if you do not make needed changes. Neighboring runes can assist you in deciphering exactly what the circumstances are.

URUZ

Upright: The upright position indicates health and strength in natural powers of resistance to ailments or aspects of life. If someone's health is the issue, it indicates a speedy recovery. This rune rules over changes of an unexpected kind, in which you need to draw upon the raw strength within you that only this rune can supply. Changes can be positive or negative.

Reversed: It warns that you have failed, or are about to fail, to take advantage of the moment and that you have shown weak power of will.

THURIAZ

Upright: This rune represents protection and luck. It can signify that unexpected good fortune is heading your way, or that the good luck you have been experiencing is about to end. The surrounding runes will tell you whether this affects a relationship, business or financial aspect, or an emotional situation.

Reversed: This is similar to what is suggested in the upright position, except that it reveals that you are unwilling to take the advice or information given in the reading. It represents your luck changing from positive to negative. You must proceed with caution.

ANSUZ

Upright: This represents the spoken word; the taking of advice or spoken wisdom. It tells you that a test of some kind challenges you, which may be written or oral. ANSUZ often signifies that the advice given by a parent, friend, or elder should be taken because it is unbiased and helpful.

Reversed: Do not believe anything you hear at the moment. Doubt all that is said to you and always get a second opinion. This position reveals lies and deceit.

RAIDHO

Upright: This is a symbol of travel. It usually suggests a journey—either a physical one, such as a flight on an airplane, or a journey of the soul. It also indicates a positive time for negotiations or needed discussion. Financially, it indicates a time to buy or sell.

Reversed: Upcoming travel can be negative and comes unexpectedly. Other people may come to visit you at a bad time. It could mean a possible problem with a transit system; a delay or an accident. You should postpone travel if the other runes reveal this possibility are coupled with RAIDHO. Plans that you have recently made may become interrupted, delayed, or otherwise upset.

KENAZ

Upright: A rune symbol of power, strength, and energy. It can indicate the need and importance of a positive attitude or change. It is a protective sign that shows worries and troubles becoming more manageable. It can indicate a good time to start something new, like a relationship or job. When concerning romance, it always represents the man in the relationship.

This rune is important to crafts-people and artists because it promotes creativity and the birth of new ideas.

Reversed: There will be a loss or an ending of some kind. It may reveal an obstacle in your progress at work, in a relationship, or other areas of your life. Concerning romance, it can signify parting and separation.

GIFU

This rune regards a partnership in either love or business and shows an important evolution within a relationship. If action is taken during the time span indicated in the reading, only the best outcome will result. Examine all surrounding runes carefully to truly find the meaning in relation to your question. A gift or act of generosity may be revealed—it may be a gift of love or a material object.

If the surrounding runes and GIFU do indicate a problem, GIFU will signify that the problem is an emotional one. GIFU has no reversed position.

WUNJO

Upright: Happiness and joy are about to enter your life. This rune is a positive omen in a runecast. It can mean success when surrounded by other positive runes. Any action you take in the situation should result in success and total happiness.

Reversed: There is a possible crisis or the onset of unhappiness. Find out what area of your life is effected by examining the surrounding runes.

HAGALL

This rune is a potent, yet enigmatic symbol. It indicates interference from an impersonal force in the seeker's life. Most often HAGALL is negative. It represents a disruption of sorts as well as obstacles or misfortune out of the seeker's control, such as a job loss or a failing relationship. However, the impersonal forces may be at work in a positive light; for example, a successful job interview in which the company management decides to hire you. HAGALL depends very much upon the surrounding runes in order to exhibit its true meaning in the runecast. Take your time and carefully study its influence with the other runes. Often, it tells you that now is not a good time to begin new projects or starts. This rune has no reverse meaning.

NIED

Upright: This is a rune of patience. It expresses that no matter how tough life may be right now, or how much you wish to resolve a problem at hand, the resolution will not occur any faster with worry and stress. You need to have patience. NIED reveals that you will pass through a difficult time of learning, perhaps a lesson of life. It may signify the need to think twice. It concentrates on your needs as opposed to your wants. *Reversed:* Reconsider any plans you have made or how you have been reacting to a situation at hand. NIED indicates you may be taking an improper course of action in a situation.

ISA

Signifies the need to put plans or ideas on hold. Now is not the right time. It often shows ill feelings may arise in a relationship of some kind—whether business, romance, family, or friendship. The runes surrounding ISA will determine what type of relationship this pertains to and may indicate separation. It can reveal disloyalty on your part or that of the other person. If the other runes are positive then the situation is resolvable, but if all the other runes indicate a negative runecast, it is too late. This rune has no reversed meaning.

JERA

Signifies rewards of a karmic nature for your efforts expended. If referring to a legal matter, this rune represents legalities and justice of all types, and depending upon the surrounding runes, will reveal if the outcome is positive or negative. This rune has no reversed meaning.

EIHWAZ

This rune indicates that you have considered a reasonable action in the situation at hand and can very well achieve your goal. It may show a slight delay or indication of trouble that will, in the end, turn out to be in your favor. This rune has no reversed meaning.

PERDHRO

Upright: This rune reigns over occult abilities and all that is hidden. It indicates that something that has been hidden will be revealed to you. Usually this is positive, such as reclaiming a lost item or developing advanced skill in your interest of an occult ability. It may signify that a secret you have tried to conceal will be uncovered. With other runes it may indicate the gift of unearned money or a surprise. It may reveal illness, or that an occult ability will help the seeker through troubled times.

Reversed: The outcome you had hoped for may not happen. Skeletons in your closet may be revealed. Financial disappointment may occur. If other runes show financial concerns, do not lend money to anyone or make an impulsive investment. It may indicate sexual problems with a romantic relationship.

EOLH

Upright: A new, fortunate influence is coming into your life, often through instinct. EOLH is a rune of friendship, it may indicate a new relationship of some kind, as well as a possible career advancement or successful move to a new place. It is a protective rune and its upright position signifies that you will be protected from bad luck and misfortune during the time indicated by the reading. It helps you heighten your instincts and ability to sense possible disaster from clues within the runecast.

Reversed: You will be vulnerable and quite possibly deceived by someone. Everything you are doing is to the benefit of someone involved, and you are not benefiting at all from the situation. Take care that you do not sacrifice yourself to others who may mislead you or abuse your good intentions. Be careful not to be deceived by yourself. This rune, when coupled with other runes, may indicate an offer that should be refused. Concerning a new relationship of love, EOLH warns to be cautious—proceed slowly until you know your new partner better.

SIGEL

This rune is almost always positive. It is a rune of victory that virtually guarantees success. Any opposition that may come your way at this time is overcome with ease. When surrounded by runes showing business or material things, it could indicate that you are overworking yourself and need to get some rest in order to avoid the perils of stress. When surrounded by runes that show a negative runecast, it indicates much worrying over problems, coupled with a lack of motivation to resolve them. This rune has no reversed meaning.

TIR

Upright: You will have success in any form of competition. It may show that you are about to fight for what you believe and that you will probably win—unless the runecast is otherwise extremely negative. You will have the power of your will to overcome odds and be triumphant. If the runecast is negative, the opposition may succeed. Concerning love and relationships, it reveals happiness and new romance. TIR is generally a masculine rune and would represent the male Querent, and indicates the strength of his will. If the seeker is female, it would indicate an important man in her life who concerns her the most. If TIR is upright, then the man is of good character and has good intentions. If TIR is reversed, approach him with caution. This rune may also show fast recovery from sickness when neighboring runes suggest it.

Reversed: In this position, TIR can indicate that you are losing enthusiasm and failing to succeed in competitive circumstances. It may reveal that you are not using your creative powers to process ideas that would help you succeed and that you are acting impatiently. For a male querent, it suggests he is ready to give up efforts when confronted with obstacles. Concerning love and romance, TIR shows that any relationship in question will not reach a definite or permanent conclusion. It signifies misunderstandings and the lack of, or trouble with, communication. Surrounding runes will help you decipher if the outcome is positive or negative.

BEORC

Upright: A rune of kinship and birth, it indicates the birth of an idea, creativity, and at times even actual child-birth. It warns for you to work through your situation with care and to be alert. Any plans in the works should be implemented immediately. Depending upon its position in the runecast, BEORC can signify a new romance, a new beginning, a new project, or some kind of beginning that will result in happiness. In a positive runecast, BEORC shows a good outcome, but in a negative runecast it indicates that your happiness or success will be brief.

Reversed: This position shows possible family problems or domestic disputes. It means that trouble is brewing or already apparent between you and those closest to you in your life. It is a warning, except when surrounded completely by negative runes that indicates destruction of relationships and possible irreconcilable differences. In either case, neighboring runes should help identify the subject of this information. In business queries, it means the venture at hand will fail, or shows temporary obstacles which will only delay matters.

EHWAZ

Upright: This rune indicates anticipated and positive change. You will make steady progress. It can mean a journey; a family reunion, moving to a new home, or travel by land. This rune usually represents physical movement and new living places. It also suggests that you are handling a problem or situation correctly and that you will obtain the desired result.

Reversed: With positive runes surrounding it, the reversed meaning of EHWAZ is exactly the same as its upright meaning. With negative runes, it suggests that you not proceed with any changes that you may be considering for the time being. If you do so, misfortune could result.

MANNAZ

Upright: This rune indicates that you will receive cooperation or needed help with the present problem from other people. It may show that you are too emotionally distressed about the matter to do anything about it and that you should listen to the advice of others. With positive runes, MANNAZ suggests that now is the time for the issuing of new plans or changes. With negative runes, it warns that you are overly stressed about the situation and are ready to give up. At times this rune suggests magical ability—the other runes will define this. Whatever the gender of the seeker, MANNAZ sometimes indicates that the seeker is having a problem dealing with women in his or her life.

Reversed: You will receive no help from people around you at this time. Cast the runes again at a later time to see if this situation has changed. Your plans and efforts will be met with challenges and obstacles. An individual or group of people may be making your life difficult and contributing to current problems. The situation could get ugly. The surrounding runes will show how to handle this dilemma and how to deal with others. In some runecasts, MANNAZ indicates that you are your own adversary. It may show that selfishness or a negative attitude is the cause of your problem. It advises you to stop being self-centered and examine the situation from another's point of view.

LAGAZ

Upright: Follow your intuition and you will receive guidance you are unaware of—perhaps from a higher source. This rune can show psychic abilities or a prophetic vision that brings your attention to the possibility of a bad offer or a bad situation. If the seeker is female, then LAGAZ, a feminine rune, will symbolize her—it signifies that she will be able to effectively deal with current troubles. If the seeker is a man, it indicates a strong woman who stands by him in the background. In a result position, LAGAZ indicates that you will be met with assistance and sympathy from those you consult for advice regarding this situation.

Reversed: Your intuition is greatly misleading you. You are trying to settle a matter for which you have no aptitude. Do not take the easy way out, however, or else it will lead to massive trouble. It can signify a woman who is bringing much trouble into your life, a back-stabbing friend, or a disloyal partner. For a man it warns the same, coupled with a warning that if he starts a new love affair it will result in utter unhappiness.

ING

This rune is always positive. You will successfully conclude the problem and prosper in any projects you wish to undertake. It may show that your anxiety over the problem will subside and relief will come, since the problem will be solved. Combined with other positive runes, ING can indicate favorable events such as the birth of a child, a new career, or a romance. It primarily denotes an end to an old cycle in your life and the birth of a new one. It signals failure only if surrounded by negative runes. This rune has no reversed meaning.

DAEG

Symbolizes growth and increase. If surrounded by negative runes, it decreases their negativity by indicating that resolution and success over obstacles is soon to come. You have the ability to turn the situation around in your favor; you must simply act now. Growth with DAEG is not sudden, but evolves slowly. You may not be aware that there are changes taking place, but in the future you will suddenly take note and all will be well. It can suggest that projecting a positive attitude will help your present situation, or that your worrying and dwelling on the situation is actually pulling the problems to you. Sometimes it indicates a new way of thinking, religious enlightenment, or a new way of living. This rune has no reverse meaning.

OTHEL

Upright: A rune that represents the things that money can buy. If money is indicated in the runecast, then OTHEL shows it arriving in a trust or inheritance situation. Depending upon what runes neighbor OTHEL, it can show if you are being too materialistic, a penny pincher, or if you are a hard worker who works diligently to fulfill your dreams and wishes. Concerning help in the current matter, old friends or elders will be your best choice.

Reversed: You are attempting to progress too quickly. If you continue, you will be met with delay and frustration. You may even totally damage the outcome of the situation. If surrounded by predominately positive runes, OTHEL shows that achievement is still possible but won't happen anytime soon. It may also show that you feel everything in life should be handed to you on a silver platter, and you would rather have this situation simply result in your favor without lifting a finger to resolve it. In financial matters it signifies much the same; do not expect financial help from anyone or any organization—you must take care of this matter yourself.

The various rune definitions given here are diverse and complex. When attempting to read a runecast, you must interpret each rune's meaning through the help of all other runes involved and carefully consider the question at hand.

Casting the Runes

Place a plain cloth on a section of the floor or a tabletop that you have designated as your magical work area. Hold all of the runes in your cupped hands, then allow them to scatter onto the area as you spread your hands apart.

Next, place all the runes in their correct alphabetical order with the symbols facing upward (See the table on page 105, which shows the Elder Futhark alphabet in its correct order.)

After this is done, you may wish to invoke one of the guardians of the runes, Odin or Freyja, to ask that the runes answer clearly and accurately and that they serve you well. This step is optional. A sample invocation might be:

> *Mighty Odin, the master of the Runes,*
> *And Freyja; Goddess of Excellence and Good,*
> *Allow me guidance of careful hands and orderly thought*
> *so that I may receive a true reading.*

You may prefer to call upon your own deity, guide, or a force that has assisted you in other spiritual and magical work.

Now, turn all the runes to face downward. Swirl them around in a clockwise motion with one or both hands. You are "shuffling" the runes just as you would a deck of cards. Continue until you are certain you do not remember where any particular rune is placed. Next, select the number of runes needed to form your runecast. (Two rune layouts are given in this chapter.) Meditate and concentrate while choosing your runes. Do not rush. Choose one at a time, placing each one in front of you, face-down and in accordance to your chosen layout. Once you have selected your runes, turn over each rune, one at a time, as if flipping the page of a book. Doing so will make certain that the runes already upright remain upright and those reversed will stay reversed. It is irrelevant whether the runes are lined up for the reading from left to right, or vice versa. To be consistent in your readings, however, it is advisable to lay them out and read them from left to right.

Two Sample Rune Layouts

Layout 1: Asking the Three Norns

We have chosen to include this layout because it is simple and allows you to begin using your runes immediately. However, there is a veritable treasure chest of possible layouts and magical uses for the runes. (Refer to the Suggested Reading section for additional source books.)

This runecast simply answers "yes" or "no," so your questions should be framed with this in mind. For example, you could ask, "Should I move to a new area?" or "Should I change my career?" or "Will I win the affections of someone I am attracted to?"

This layout is aptly called "Asking the Three Norns." Individually, the Norns are known as Urdhr, Verthani, and Skuld—past, present, and future.[6] They represent all knowledge and are special patrons of the art of divination.[7]

The Norns will answer quickly and accurately; however, they cannot answer multiple questions such as, "When will I find employment and will I be happy with my job?" This is actually two questions, not one, and makes answering "yes" or "no" difficult.

Once the question has been established, concentrate on it for a moment. Make sure that your question is clearly stated and firmly focused in your mind.

Cast your runes as instructed above and select three for this reading. They should be laid in front of you with the first on the left, the second in the middle, and the third to your right. Turn the runes over and note how many are upright and how many are reversed. The upright runes indicate a positive influence; the reversed indicate a negative influence. Runes that have no reversed meaning require an understanding of their potential positive or negative influences with regard to your particular question. These runes are easily influenced by neighboring runes that help ascertain their meaning.

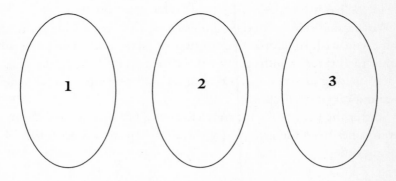

Rune Divination Layout 1. Asking the Three Norns.

If all the runes are of a positive nature, the answer is a definite yes. All negative runes are a definite no. If the three runes are a combination of positive and negative, you will have to investigate their meaning and work to gain an intelligible answer. Two positive and one negative indicate that although the answer is yes, there is an aspect of the situation that will not fulfill your expectations—in other words, there may be a catch. Study the meaning of each rune and use their particular positions—upright, reversed, or non-reversible—to obtain a clear "yes" or "no" answer in cases where there is no immediate certainty. If two runes are negative and one is positive, the answer is no, but it indicates that the seeker may not come out of the situation as badly as they might have otherwise. Two negative runes combined with a non-reversible rune almost always negates any positive attributes the non-reversible rune might indicate—this answer should be taken as a definite no.

Layout 2: Mimir's Head Seven Rune Method

This method derives its name from the oracular head of the god Mimir, which Odin himself consulted in times of trouble.[8]

Mimir's Head allows you to obtain more information from a runecast regarding what events may have led to your present dilemma and how best to deal with the situation. Mimir's Head shows events that have occurred three months past and events that will occur three months into the future. In this runecast, you are not limited to asking "yes" or "no" questions. You might ask Mimir's Head, "What will happen if I...," or "What can I do about..."

While using this method, you must be specific regarding the time frame you wish to address; your question may concern the present rather than three months past or three months into the future. This is fine as long as you concentrate upon a current time frame while focusing on your question.

Scatter the runes on your rune cloth or a flat surface, and choose seven runes from the group. Lay them out, one at a time in the following order:

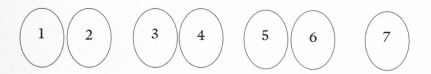

Rune Divination Layout 2. Mimir's Head Seven Rune Method

Once the runes have been turned faced up, you will read the first two runes together. These two runes represent the problem at hand. Reading two runes at once is tricky until you know each individual rune well, but following their definitions and using your intuition will help. Attempt to combine the meanings of the two runes, or consider what traits both have in common. Do not become frustrated if you cannot do this immediately; patience and careful study will surely aid your understanding and result in a better reading. Runes that are difficult to read together are usually the ones with the most insightful information. Consider such questions as: are both runes indicating gain for the seeker? Do both runes indicate a delay for the seeker? Even if one rune is positive and the other negative, each will somehow illuminate the meaning of the other.

The runes in positions three and four are also read as a pair and show what outside factors, usually in the past, have led to the present situation. At times they will indicate factors that the seeker may not have realized or considered, and thus help bring resolution to the situation.

The runes in positions five and six are also read as a pair, and are the most important runes in the entire runecast. These runes show how the situation may best be handled. Take care to thoroughly examine and interpret the meaning of these runes. They might suggest that the seeker should wait and not act immediately, or simply "go around" the problem instead of dealing with it. Such a result might indicate that the seeker is dwelling on something that is not as threatening or urgent as it is thought to be.

The seventh position will indicate the result. It should be read in conjunction with the other six runes—not by itself. For example, if NIED is in the seventh position, it may mean "no" in a negative runecast and "yes, but not yet," in a positive one.

From these instructions, you might think that Mimir's Head is an easy layout for reading the runes. In practice, however, you may find it to be a challenge. Patience and careful examination of all rune definitions are key.

Endnotes

1. Lisa Peschel, *A Practical Guide To The Runes: Their Uses In Divination And Magick*, (St. Paul: Llewellyn Publications, 1989), 15.
2. Tony Willis, *The Runic Workbook*, (New York: Sterling Publishing Company, 1990), 37.
3. Ibid., 37.
4. Ibid, 37.
5. Ibid, 38.
6. Peschel, *A Practical Guide to the Runes*, 30.
7. Ibid, 30.
8. Willis, *The Runic Workbook*, 81.

7

Medicine and Magical Shield Construction and Use

There are several types of medicine shields and magical shields used in contemporary pagan practices. For the purposes of this book, we will concentrate on the construction of a medicine wheel shield, which is used by many Shamanic traditions, and the magical shield used by many pagan religious traditions. The construction of both shields is similar, although their uses are quite different.

The medicine wheel shield is used for healing oneself, other individuals and creatures, and our environment. This implement plays a significant role in Native American shamanic practice, and has maintained an important role in healing work of all types, whether mental, emotional, physical, or spiritual. The primary function of such a shield is protection, but it can also be used to indicate the principles of one's religious or magical path, to conjure dreams, or to heal. In ancient shamanic practices, shields were also used to help form a bond between a shaman and a particular totem, such as an animal totem.[1] In addition, shamans use the shield to record important events by drawing pictures, symbols, and words upon the shield.

Sometimes the medicine shield hangs on the front door of a house to signify that a healer resides within. In Europe, remnants of this ancient tradition can be found in the shields of the various guilds of artisans that were hung from the May tree in the center of the village.[2] The reason for this was to alert strangers or newcomers what skills, professions, and medicines were available in that particular village.[3]

The magical shield can be used in much the same way as the medicine shield. However its primary function is more significant in the magical arts. The magical shield is most often used in pagan magical practices to shield the practitioner from negative energy or to project positive energy toward the stated goal of the ceremony. At times it is used in conjunction with the techniques of dance and chant to build energy for the cone of power.

Shield Construction

Materials Needed

The following is a list of items needed for the construction of a shield. You may substitute or add decoration you feel is appropriate for your personal shield:

- Plain leather, animal hide, cloth, or fabric measuring 2' by 2' (or larger if you desire a larger shield)

- Colored string, thread, yarn, or leather strips

- A hoop (obtained at craft supply stores or shops that carry cross-stitch and embroidery supplies). Chose any size hoop you want to work with. For a more natural shield you can use a willow branch to make a hoop.

- A sewing needle and neutral colored thread
- An assortment of paints, colored pens, or markers
- Stones or pebbles
- Feathers, bells, colored ribbon, or any other decorative items
- Scissors

Using a Commercial Hoop

Step 1 *Acquiring a hoop.*
You may use a commercial hoop purchased at a craft store to create the body of the shield.

Step 2 *Stretching the fabric.*
Take the animal hide, cloth, or fabric, and stretch it over the hoop so that it completely covers the center of the hoop.

Step 3 *Securing the fabric.*
Secure the material around the hoop by placing the fabric between the inner and outer hoops. The fixed tack of the hoop locks the fabric in place.

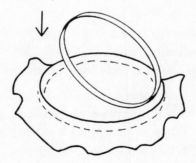

Step 3. Secure the fabric around the commercial hoop by placing the fabric between the inner and outer hoops.

Using a Natural Wood Hoop

Step 1   *Creating a hoop.*
If you are using a willow branch to create a hoop, bend the branch ends together to create a hoop the size you need and tie them securely with string, thread, or yarn. If you have excess wood from the ends of the branch sticking out of the tied section, break or cut the ends.

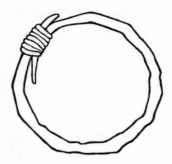

Step 1. To create a natural hoop, use a willow branch. Gently bend it into a circle and tie the ends securely with string.

Step 2   *Stretching the fabric.*
Take the animal hide or selected fabric, and stretch it over the hoop so that it completely covers the center of the hoop.

Step 3   *Securing the fabric.*
Tack the fabric into place with a needle and a strong thread or yarn. When beginning to sew, start on the underside of the shield, on the inside of the hoop.

Note: Tie a knot in the end of the thread before you begin to sew around the hoop. This will anchor the thread at the first insertion of the needle. Bring the needle and thread over the outside of the hoop and back under to the inside of the hoop so that you are wrapping the hoop with the thread over the fabric. Continue sewing all the way around the hoop.

Finish sewing with the needle extending out the back (underside) of the shield. Remove the needle from the remaining thread and tie a knot to secure it. If you are making a leather shield, you'll want to use a heavy needle and sinew or thin leather thong.

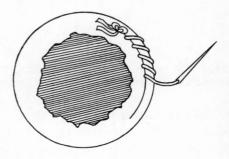

Step 3. Secure the fabric around the hoop using a heavy thread or leather thong.

Decorating Your Shield

Step 1   *Applying Decoration.*
The difficult part of crafting your shield is now finished. You are now free to apply decoration to the front of the shield. Use paints, felt tip pens, or colored markers to apply your symbols, drawings, or decorative art to the main body of the shield material (diagram 1, page 132).

If you are planning to use the shield for healing magic, certain symbolism, such as the colors you normally work with or even the words from an actual spell, can be worked into a decorative design. If your shield is meant to serve as a protective device while you work magic, any protective images you wish to apply, such as rune symbols, would be ideal.

Step 1. Use paints, felt tip pens, or colored markers to apply symbols, drawings, or decorative art to the body of your shield.

Step 2 *Finishing touches.*

Feathers, bells, colored ribbon, and other ornaments should be applied last. These complimentary adornments are meaningful attributes that should represent your practice.

You can apply feathers to the shield by tying a leather strip to the end point of the feather's quill. Poke a hole in the edge of your shield material, pull the leather strip through, and secure it.

You may choose to sew the quill onto the shield, especially if you use ribbon or yarn. Bells hung from colored ribbon make a nice musical addition to any shield.

Decorating options are limitless. Allow your creativity to awaken with this project.

Many different designs for the shield are possible. We once crafted an Egyptian-style shield for a Wiccan friend. The shield had miniature silver and gold pentagrams and ankhs dangling on colored ribbons from the bottom of the shield. Another time, we constructed a medicine shield and used colored threads to sew dried herbs onto the body of the shield, which was made of deer skin.

✦   ✦   ✦

Shield Uses

In describing how to make a shield, we combined instructions for both the medicine wheel shield and the magical shield. Here we will describe the use of both shields within various pagan religions and magical practice. The two shields may be used separately for their traditional purposes or one's personal shield can be used for both a medicine shield and magical shield.

The shield is typically used during ceremonies or healing sessions; its owner wears it like the shield of a warrior or simply holds it up in front of them.[4] Shamanic shields are primarily used for healing, whereas other pagan traditions use the shield for healing and clearing sacred space of negative energies or beings. There are a host of ways to use a shield. You may even discover other uses that are uniquely your own.

A Healing Spell

This healing spell shows how a medicine or magical shield might be used in spell casting.

As the circle is being cast, take up your shield in one hand and hold it facing away from you, toward the outside of your circle or sacred space. Slowly walk around the diameter of your circle. Hold the shield out to line up with the edge of your circle to purify before the spell is performed. As you walk slowly clockwise, state the following:

> *Round the circle I consecrate thee;*
> *with a shield against all wickedness and evil.*
> *I shall preserve and bless the power raised within thee;*
> *In the names of the Old Ones, So Mote It Be!*

As you walk around the circle with the shield extended in front of you, shake it as if to symbolically frighten away any evil spirits or negative energy hanging around your sacred space. (Bells attached to the shield are especially effective for this purpose; the ringing sound will certainly help in dispelling unwanted energy or guests!)

Once you have circled your area completely, place the shield on the altar or on the ground. Next, use your ritual staff or wand to invoke the four elements and your deity.

After the invocation, announce to your deity, and any other natural forces you may use during magical work, the following

> *I have come this night to perform a healing spell to banish the illness within the body of* (state the person's name), *and assist them in healing of mind and body.*

You may have a specific healing technique that you like to use. Some people employ candle magic, some only use visualization, while others use color magic. Choose whatever healing method works best for you.

Once the healing magic has been conducted and the needed energy raised,[5] hold the shield in your protective hand, which in many cases is the right hand, and infuse your shield with the energy you have collected. Holding your shield upright toward the heavens, release the energy through the shield. You would normally use your staff, wand, or ritual knife for this, but if your shield was specifically made for healing work then use it instead. Upon release of those energies say the following:

> *Unto thee* (name of recipient), *is health and strength threefold; taken within thy body to serve and build thee.*
> *The healing magic shall do its deed;*
> *So Mote It Be!*

After this, put down your shield and continue grounding yourself. You may sit upon the ground and meditate with your shield in hand. This will help absorb any remaining energies from you and speed your body chemistry back to its normality.

Using your shield as a tool in meditation, especially in the contemplation of an issue or decision, can assist in efforts to shift your consciousness since it is visually stimulating to your mind. The decorations you choose to adorn your shield reflect your spiritual and magical practices, personality, and outlook on life. They create a map of your innermost beliefs. Looking within the shield, you look within yourself. Your shield can reveal unforeseen aspects of yourself and show you how to handle certain situations. It may present negative traits you were previously unaware of that are creating much trouble in your life, or it can reflect the golden light of goodness and the proper action you should take in response to an unpleasant situation.

Your shield can be used as a divination tool; it is uniquely created by you for your personal use. The shield is a magical device that acts in a similar way to a black mirror used in divination—gazing into its design opens the channels of your mind. This can awaken your psychic faculties of contemplation, consideration, and resolution—factors necessary to pull yourself through the hardships of life.

Chapter 11 focuses on meditation and consecration of all the ritual tools listed in this book. Consider using your newly created shield in one of the exercises provided. You'll be very pleased with the insights you can gain by using your shield. It can provide an unveiling glimpse into your inner self and help in achieving the goals you strive for in life.

Endnotes

1. A totem is an animal, a plant, or some other natural object which is the emblem of a clan family, or tribe of traditional peoples and sometimes revered as its founder, ancestor, or guardian.
2. Lorler, *Shamanic Healing*, 194.
3. Ibid., 194.
4. Ibid, 194.
5. See Chapter 3 for exercises to raise energy.

8

Carving, Painting, and Wood Branding

Once you have created your ritual tool, you will want to apply symbolism to it that reflects your personal religious or magical path. Each of the methods described here are excellent techniques for achieving this.

Carving

Woodcarving is an ancient tradition. Carvings and sculptures have been found buried in the Egyptian desert, some dating back to 2,000 B.C.E. Eleven wooden relief panels found in Egypt in A.D. 1860, preserved by the drifting sands for over 4,000 years, are believed to be the oldest in the world.[1]

Examples of carved wood can be found in many cultures from ancient Greece to medieval Europe. Greek wood carvers were apparently influenced by their Egyptian counterparts. The Greeks carved wooden statues depicting Greek Gods with human features—naked figures with smiling expressions.

Woodcarving reached the height of popularity during the Gothic Period (A.D. 1180-1540). Magnificently intricate altars and reliefs were carved for cathedrals throughout Europe, many of which are still intact.

While still popular in the late 20th century, woodcarving is now used more for smaller sculptures and projects than for extensive interior decorating.

In ages past, primitive carving or traditional woodcarving were prevalent practices. Hieroglyphics carved upon reliefs, doors, and furnishings of Egypt are fine examples of the ancient art of woodcarving. In modern times, rural people young and old sell handcrafted wooden bowls, cups, and staffs along the highway. They are the modern heirs of a venerable custom who carry on the art of woodcarving often handed down as a family tradition.

From ancient times to the modern era, woodcarving has continued to be a popular method of creating magical items, religious tools, and sacred furnishings.

Compared to other kinds of carving, woodcarving is relatively slow. However, the gradual development of a carving may give you a sense of connection with the past—you may feel a bond with the woodcarvers of medieval Europe or ancient Egypt. In addition, carving personal symbolism on your ritual staff, ritual knife, or other implement is truly rewarding because it is considered a more "pure" process (in an artistic sense) of applying symbolism to wood—rather than adding additional substances like paint to the wood or using hot irons to brand symbols into the wood surface. The process of carving is based on the principle of sculpting the wood itself.

Woodcarving is a skill that is separate from carpentry and cabinetmaking. It is usually considered an art or fine craft and is generally not taught in trade schools. In fact, most woodcarving skill is passed directly from master to student. An expert carpenter or cabinetmaker usually does not know the art of woodcarving unless self-taught. Professional craftspeople today use modern tools, such as electric carving machines that have steel or carbide bits, to carve furniture and other household accessories.

Carving Symbolism on Your Wood

Step 1   *Chose your carving tools.*

Woodcarving can be done by anyone using several different tools. A chisel, gouge, sharp non-serrated knife such as a pocket knife or a Swiss army knife, or one of the commercially available carving kits may be used.

Initial carving of the design's pattern into the wood will be done with the knife. More advanced carving will be done with the chisel and gouge. Remember, a chisel makes straight cuts into the wood, whereas a gouge cuts grooves. You should only use a gouge or a chisel on a project once you have mastered these tools. Practice makes perfect. If you have never carved before, practice on a piece of scrap wood to find the tool and technique that best suits you. Once you carve a piece of wood, it is very difficult to undo.

Every woodcarver has a method as unique as the individual. There is no set procedure to follow. You must teach yourself through patience and perseverance. Using different tools will result in different carving effects; practice with several tools until you create your own desired effect.

Step 2   *Drawing your design.*

Always draw your symbolism on the wood surface with a pencil first. This serves as a pattern for your work and is much easier to change than the actual carving. If you plan to widen the lines and angles of your symbols or make them more pronounced, be careful not to draw them close together (diagram 2, page 140)

Step 3   *Securing your wood.*

When carving your ritual tool, secure the piece in a vise or fasten it to your work table using a C-clamp. This allows you to use both hands while you work.

Step 2. Draw your selected symbolism on the wood surface with a pencil before you begin to carve.

Step 4   *Initial carving.*

Use a sharp carving tool to etch out the penciled design you have sketched on your wood. Place the knife point, or carving tool of choice, against the penciled drawing. Hold the handle of the tool with one hand and use a hammer or the palm of your free hand to tap its handle.

If the wood begins to splinter during this process, as it certainly will if you carve against the wood grain, do not panic. Simply continue to carve. Once the woodcarving is completed, sanding will eliminate any splintering.

Step 4. Use a knife or chisel and follow the pattern you've drawn on your wood block.

Step 5   *"Fleshing-out" your design.*

After etching the outline of the pattern, widen the carvings with a gouge or chisel. A gouge will give you a round groove, while the chisel will provide a flat groove. Use these tools as you did the knife, applying force with your palm or a hammer. Start gently, gradually increasing the pressure until you reach the desired effect. Take your time and proceed carefully.

Relief Carving

Carving a flat wooden surface is also called relief carving. Technically, a carved relief is the projection of figures or forms from a flat background. Any flat pattern or symbolism can be used to create a relief carving. A relief carving is closer in appearance to a textured painting rather than a three-dimensional work such as a carved figure or statue.

There are three types of relief carving. In high relief, the degree of projection of the figure from the wood surface is high and very three-dimensional—almost detached from the background. In low relief, the projection of the figure from the background wood is very slight. In both high and low relief, the background surface of the wood around the figure is cut away to varying depths. More background wood is cut away in a high relief than in a low relief. Sunk relief is a type of carving in which the background wood around the figures is not cut away to form a background plane. Instead, the highest points of the carving are level with the surface into which the carving has been cut.[2] Whichever type of relief carving you choose depends upon how much background wood you wish to cut away.

Anubis. An example of sunk relief carving.

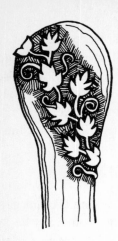

Ivy on a ritual staff.
An example of decorative carving.

Relief Carving.
Serpent wand

The depth of the carving into the wood's surface and the initial design itself can provide a three-dimensional appearance to any relief carving. For example, the Egyptian God Anubis can be carved into a ritual tool by using a flat design carefully etched into the wood surface. If the outline of Anubis is made progressively deeper into the wood, it can appear as a three-dimensional figure almost free from the background. The illustration of the relief carving of Anubis shown on the previous page is a sunk relief. The figure of Anubis is on the same level as the background—except for the wood immediately next to the outline of the figure, no background wood has been removed.

The technique of relief carving creates interesting and beautiful results. For instance, a ritual staff can appear to have a vine twisting around its length and leaves of ivy hugging its form. This is achieved by carving deep enough to create the three-dimensional illusion that the ivy is separated from the actual staff. The wand displayed on the cover of this book, with a carved serpent, is another example of this.

Certain tools work best for this technique, and the gouge is one of them. The gouge is wonderful for creating depth. It also produces a suitable width for the carving pattern.

Do not become frustrated or impatient at your first attempt at woodcarving. This difficult art requires practice. After learning and using these techniques, you will be able to carve Gods, Goddesses, people, animals, mythical creatures, flowers, and an endless array of designs. Patience is the key.

Some books on woodcarving are listed in the Suggested Reading section at the end of this book.

Painting

Painting is an ancient art. Twenty-five thousand years ago Paleolithic humankind pictured fertility and hunting rituals involving animals and the Hunting God in cave paintings, which still exist.[3] You can enjoy painting the symbolism unique to your spiritual path and magical life experiences, just as our ancestors did when painting their religious images inside caves.

Painting Your Ritual Tool

Painting is a self-taught art, although many art supply stores and skilled artists offer lessons. There are countless techniques for applying paint, various kinds of paint that can be used, and numerous types of brushes and painting tools available to obtain desired effects. Here, we will concentrate only on the most basic painting method.

Step 1   *Choosing paint and brushes.*

Although any type of paint may be used, we recommend acrylic. Its color is vibrant, it is easy to remove and clean up, and it is perfect for both beginners and advanced painters. The ideal brush to use with any paint is the sable brush, a natural hair brush which is available at paint dealers, hobby shops, or craft stores. Natural hair brushes work best, since the stiffness of synthetic brushes makes it harder to apply the paint. Remember that the smaller the brush, the finer the lines of paint.

Practice on scrap wood first. Unlike a painter's canvas, wood is porous and varies in surface texture. See how your paint is absorbed and how it sets on your chosen wood type. Apply different degrees of paint thickness and various strokes of the brush or paint marker. Practice until you achieve the effect you want.

Step 2   *Sanding.*

It is important to remember that if you plan to paint your ritual tool, you must sand the wood first. There is no need to use wood stain if you plan on painting the implement— use a primer coat of paint instead.

Note: Never apply stain over paint; the stain will drastically change the color of the painted symbolism. Should this happen, you can remove the stain by sanding, but the paint will be removed as well. If you plan to varnish or shellac your project, painting should be done first.

Step 3   *Application.*

Acrylic paint may be applied right out of the tube, or it may be thinned with water. Sketch your design onto the wood first, and then paint it. Two or three coats may be needed, to ensure that your design is even in color. Acrylics dry quickly, so additional coats may be applied after about fifteen minutes.

Step 4   *Optional finishing step.*

If you want to add a protective coat of finish to your ritual tool, follow the instructions for applying varnish, shellac, or lacquer given in chapter 9.

Brushes used with acrylic paint are cleaned with soap and water. All water-based paints clean up easily as long as the paint has not hardened. If the paint has hardened, brushes should be soaked in rubbing alcohol to loosen the dried paint.

Paint Markers

If using a brush seems daunting, paint dealers and craft stores also carry paint markers. These are ideal for the beginner. Paint markers are held like a pen, but apply paint instead of ink. The paint is applied easily on the wood and does not smudge like pen ink. These markers come in a variety of colors, and some contain glitter for a dazzling effect.

Ink Markers

Felt tip markers and pens can be used to apply symbolism to the wood, however, these tend to appear smudged as they are absorbed into the grain. Markers and various inks may also smear before drying, and only sanding can remove the mess. Unless you sand the wood surface to a fine smoothness before you apply a marker, a felt tip pen will make your symbols look as if they had been drawn by a child.

While markers and pens can make an adequate representation of your symbols, it is preferable to use paint.

Wood Branding

Wood branding produces rich black burn marks and imprints that cannot be achieved with other techniques such as staining, carving, or painting. It provides a truly unique, eye-catching style.

We were introduced to the art of wood branding in 1993 when we met a young couple at a Samhain (Halloween) festival who practiced a Celtic religious tradition. The man, dressed in Celtic garb, carried a magnificent oak staff covered with vivid black markings depicting symbols from the Celtic Ogham alphabet. We inquired as to how he achieved the this effect, and he informed us that he had used a hand-held solder iron to apply them to the wood. We were intrigued. We had never considered burning or branding symbols into our ritual tools. Soon after, we purchased a solder iron and enjoyed learning this simple technique for wood branding.

A solder iron is a pointed metal tool heated for use in melting and applying solder. It may be purchased at hardware stores or home centers. Solder is a metal alloy (a mixture of two or more metals), used to join or patch metal parts or surfaces. Depending upon the manufacturer, this device may also be called a soldering gun.

It is interesting how this tool, which works with metals, can be used on wood. When employed for woodworking, the soldering iron is used without solder. Follow the steps detailed on the next pages to easily brand your wood

Branding Symbolism on Your Wood

Step 1 *Heating the solder iron.*

This tool is heated electrically. Plug it into an electrical outlet and wait a few minutes until the iron is hot enough to be used.

Step 2 *Burning the design.*

Hold the tip of the solder iron close to the wood's surface. Do not apply pressure until you can judge how close the tip must be to produce a burn. The burn will appear as a very fine, black speck. You can literally write or draw with the solder iron to produce your symbol or design. Although this technique is rather simple, we suggest practicing on scrap wood first.

Step 2. Hold the tip of the solder iron close to the surface of the wood and write or draw your chosen symbols.

Safety Tips for Wood Branding

Using the solder iron will not cause the wood to ignite into flames unless the iron is held directly on the wood for a long time. It is possible, however, to burn your skin, clothing, and surroundings, so use common sense when handling a hot iron. Always unplug this device when interrupted or when finished. This assures that the iron will not cause fire or burns. The iron must be laid on a safe, heat-resistant surface until cool.

Endnotes

1. Freda Skinner, *Wood Carving* (New York: Bonanza Books, MCMLXI), 110-112.
2. James Pierce. *From Abacus to Zeus.* (Englewood Cliffs, NJ: Prentice Hall, Inc., 1968), 51.
3. Raymond Buckland, *Buckland's Complete Book Of Witchcraft,* (St. Paul: Llewellyn Publications, 1990), 2.

9

Wood Fillers, Stains, Finishes, and Enamels

This chapter deals with some of the final touches that you may wish to use in the creation of your ritual tools. All of the materials mentioned here are optional, however. Wood fillers may be needed if the wood of your tool has large pores, holes, or cracks. Filling these holes is an intermediate step that is done after the tool has been created, but before any symbolism or decoration is applied. Staining, finishing, and enameling are all final steps in the completion of wooden items. Stain is a liquid substance applied especially to wood that penetrates the surface and imparts a rich color. Enamel is a paint that dries to a hard coating and can be used to cover your entire ritual tool with any color desired. A finish is a clear, protective coat; it is the last treatment or coating of a wood surface. Varnishes, shellacs, and lacquers are common finishes which are used to cover enameled, stained, decorated, or even raw wood. Whether or not you decide to use any of these substances on your ritual tool is entirely up to you.

Wood Fillers

Open-grained woods, such as oak, maple, rosewood, and mahogany, may require wood fillers. To obtain a smooth finish for your wood, you need a smooth wood surface. No matter how much you sand these woods, you will not achieve a glossy surface—if that is your goal. If stain and finish are part of your ritual tool design, and you do not mind dark, uneven splotches that will appear in open-grain texture, then you may choose to skip this procedure. At times the dark "dotted effect" from stain on open-grained wood is attractive and makes the wood appear "antiqued."

Fillers are used to close pores and fill crevices that are resistant to sanding. Once filled, the surface is sanded one last time before applying stain or finish. Commercial wood fillers are available in two forms—liquid and paste.

Liquid Wood Fillers

Liquid filler is easy to use, but it is best for projects requiring little filling. When purchasing liquid filler, ask a store employee what brush is best suited for it. Brushes come in a variety of sizes with both natural hair and synthetic bristles. Some work better than others for certain projects.

Step 1   *Application.*
Brush the filler on with a soft paint brush. Allow it to dry completely.

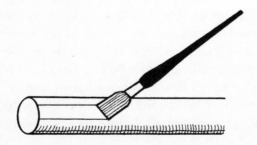

Step 1. Apply the liquid wood filler to your wood with a soft paint brush.

Step 2   *Sanding.*

After the wood filler has dried completely, sand it. Sanding removes the excess and smooths the filler that has been absorbed into crevices.

Paste Wood Fillers

Many professional woodworkers find that the paste fillers work so well that they don't bother with liquid fillers at all. The best paste fillers contain a varnish-type ingredient rather than a drying component, such as linseed oil. Ideally, paste fillers should also contain gypsum or silex, which is a form of silica. Paste fillers are neutral in color, and may be tinted with special pigments before application. Choose pigments that will match your wood color or stain.

Paste fillers work very well for large cracks or craters in the wood surface. As the wood dries, these inherent problems can present themselves. However, no filler—whether liquid or paste—can improve rotten wood.

Step 1   *Thinning and adding pigment.*

Paste fillers are usually too thick to be applied directly out of the can. You must thin the filler with benzene or turpentine naphtha before applying it to your wood. When selecting a product, be sure to read the instructions on the can. Thinning should result in a creamy material. Pigment may be added to the filler at this time.

Step 2   *Application.*

Use a stiff brush to apply the paste filler and work with the grain. Apply pressure to the brush to insure that the filler penetrates the grain. Apply a generous second coat while the first coat is still wet. Brush across the grain during the second coat.

Step 3   *Removing excess filler.*

Pay attention to the filler. It will quickly change from a wet appearance to a sudden dullness. Once it has dulled, immediately scrape off the excess immediately—if left too long, the filler will be too dry to remove. Carefully scrape across the grain with a knife to remove excess. All remaining filler permeates the grooves and cracks on the surface.

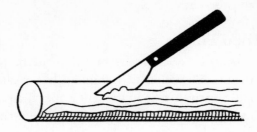

Step 3. Use a knife to scrape excess filler from the surface of your wood immediately following application.

Step 4   *Smoothing the filler.*

After scraping, use a rough cloth like burlap to massage the wood, applying pressure. Working against the grain, rub down the whole piece of wood. Next, take a soft clean cloth and work with the grain to remove smudges.

Step 4. Smooth the filler on your wood by rubbing the wood with a rough cloth, always working against the grain.

Step 5 *Drying.*

Allow your project to set overnight in a warm, dry place. The following day examine it, and determine if another coat of filler is necessary. Each coat must be allowed to dry for twenty-four hours.

Step 6 *Sanding.*

No fillers can smooth wood entirely. The applied finish does that job. When filler has dried and the surface is filled to your satisfaction, sand the wood gently with a fine sand-paper—150 grit should work well. Be careful not to sand away the filler and leave blotches, or you will have to apply another coat.

Stain

You may decide that your wood's natural color is unsatisfactory. Perhaps you want a darker or lighter tint. How do you achieve this? Staining is the answer. The stain must be applied before the finish.

Stain alters the color of the wood, but it does not seal or protect it. It should highlight, not hide, the grain and should enhance the natural color or make the wood resemble whichever wood type you desire, such as cherry or walnut. If you are working with cherry, walnut, or redwood, it is not necessary to use stain since these woods are already rich with striking natural color.

Take time to study a color chart of wood stains, which you can find at any home center or hardware store. It is also a good idea to stain a scrap piece of your wood before applying the stain to your project. Stain may look appealing in the can but undesirable on your ritual tool. Wet stain looks different than dry stain, as stains will dry darker than they appear when first applied wet. A few minutes after application, you will wipe off the excess stain with a clean, dry cloth. The longer you leave a stain on your project, the darker it will dry. If you wipe off the excess stain and want a darker finish on your staff, continue applying layers of stain until you achieve the desired effect.

Always sand the wood before staining. All stains must be allowed to dry thoroughly—eight to twenty-four hours—before a finish, such as lacquer, is applied.

There are many different types of stain to choose from. Several are listed on the following pages.

Jelled Wiping Stain

Considered foolproof, this stain is best for the beginner to use because the preparation, application, and clean up are all very simple due to its jelly-like consistency. Other stains require careful application and several steps to avoid streaks and over-applying. Using a cloth or dry pad, rub the stain onto the wood surface until it is evenly coated. Allow this to dry. Simple!

This stain is easy to use, allows for complete color control, and is the best stain for projects mentioned in this book.

Pigmented Oil Stain

Pigmented oil stain works best on softwoods, such as pine or poplar. Look for the word "wiping" on the label when you purchase pigmented oil stains. These stains cover the wood with a colored film and penetrate the pores. Stick to the simplest of these stains, which are applied with a cloth. For open-grained wood, or wood with irregularities, the stain will enhance the flaws and not penetrate as well. This lack of deep penetration into the wood surface is fine, however, if you desire a lighter color on your wood. In addition, some people find the natural flaws of the wood to be aesthetically pleasing.

If the stain you apply is too dark, you can thin the stained wood surface by gradually applying small doses of turpentine with a cloth over the surface.

Penetrating Oil Stains

Penetrating oil stains are easy to use and excellent for hardwoods. They allow the grain to come through to a greater degree than pigmented oil stains. Very often, wood stained with this material does not have to be finished any further. As it penetrates, it creates a transparent finish that is appealing.

One word of caution—these stains are difficult to remove once applied. Removal can only be accomplished by deep sanding. This is the only disadvantage to their use.

To apply a penetrating oil stain, use a brush and work with the grain. Allow the stain to dry for twenty minutes, then remove excess stain by gently wiping with a clean cloth or sponge. Do not dampen this cloth with water. Color depth can be controlled by wiping off excess stain before or after the twenty minute time limit. If you want only a slight amount of color, wipe the stain off after a minute or two. Do not allow penetrating oil stains to set completely before wiping.

Water-based Stain

Water-based stains work best on commercially purchased wood. Because the water in the stain will raise the grain of the wood, you will have to do additional sanding.

The stain is purchased in powder form and must be mixed with water. Instructions will be on the container, but the usual formula is one ounce of powder to one quart of hot water. You can mix all of the stain, bottle it, and store.

To apply, first dampen the wood with a wet sponge to raise the grain, then wait for the wood to dry. Sand lightly. This will decrease the amount of grain that the stain will raise. Brush the stain onto the wood. Use long, even strokes and be certain to work with the grain. Blot the brush to remove excess stain and continue to apply until the wood is coated evenly. The brush will pick up any excess stain on the wood. Avoid applying the stain unevenly or over-coating. Both will result in irregular dark areas. Immediately after applying, wipe gently with a clean cloth until you obtain an even color and no streaks.

Non-grain-raising Stain (NGR)

This type of stain works best on commercially purchased close-grained woods, such as birch, and wood without open pores. It does not work well on softwoods. This stain is unique since it may be sprayed or brushed onto wood. Although the name is reassuring, NGR stains will raise the grain slightly if applied with a brush rather than sprayed.

NGR stains are expensive when compared to other stains mentioned. Compared to water-based stains, they dry faster and darker and are not as vivid in color.

Apply this stain in two or three light coats. Light coats ensure better control of the color than heavier coats. Practice on scrap pieces of your wood first. If you apply coats with a brush, wipe the surface immediately with a clean cloth. A spray gun is recommended for the best application.

Staining Tips

Here are some staining tips to help overcome problems you might encounter:

- Sanding is the most important step toward achieving beautiful results. It must be done before stain is applied. Sand the wood to as smooth a texture as possible.

- Softwoods, such as pine, absorb stain a little unevenly. Be cautious when applying.

- Carvings will take stain in a manner that is dark and uneven compared to the rest of your wood. This cannot be resolved, but is not a problem since carvings are usually enhanced by it. If you feel that excessive stain has collected in a carving, wipe or blot the carving with a clean dry cloth. This will absorb extra stain and lighten the color.

- A sponge or folded piece of cheesecloth is better than a paintbrush for applying stain. If the stain's instructions recommend a brush, however, then use a brush. Brush stain onto wood in small sections, working with the grain, and press lightly to penetrate the wood. Keep a clean cloth at your side to blot running stain.

- When staining, place your ritual tool on a horizontal surface, such as a table or the floor. Cover your work area with newspapers to avoid messes. A vise or C-clamps aid in holding the project firmly in place, freeing both your hands for working. Turn the piece as you work on it. If you must apply stain vertically, start from the bottom and work upward to avoid runs.

- Initial staining should be done on the least noticeable areas on your project. If the stain is undesirable it can be removed by dabbing a cloth in diluted bleach and water and carefully wiping it away.

Finish

This is not a necessary step in the creation of your ritual tool, but we have included it for those readers who wish to have a clear, glossy finish to their project. Finishes are used much like stains, and with the exception of shellac, most finishes are made from synthetics. Shellac is natural and is formulated from the resin taken from insects.

You must decide what type of product you wish to use to finish your wood: lacquer, shellac, varnish, or oil finish. There are spraying or brushing lacquers, clear or orange tinted shellac, and natural or synthetic varnishes and oils. Some finishes are made specifically for indoor or outdoor use. If you plan to use your ritual tool primarily outdoors, then an outdoor type is best suited for your project.

Each type of finish has its own unique result. Varnish and shellac bring out the grain. Shellac, the most commonly used finish, looks very attractive, but is not durable. Lacquer is very durable and will produce a mirror-like finish. Wax causes a deep, mellow finish. Oil finishes take weeks to dry completely and do not yield any better result than finishes that are easier to use.

Finishes must be applied to your project as specified on container instructions. Most are applied by spraying or with a paint brush. Many come in spray cans.

Even clear varnishes, shellacs, and lacquers may darken the color of your wood slightly. You may wish to purchase a "non-yellowing" finish, such as "non-yellowing acrylic lacquer," to avoid this.

We recommend you speak with a knowledgeable source—a home center or lumber yard employee—to determine the finish best suited for your type of wood. Some woods look better if finished with a particular product.

We do not finish our ritual tools, whether for ourselves or for someone else, unless a client insists upon it. Not only is finish unnecessary for such projects, but as the finish seals and protects, it has a tendency to trap energies in the wood that are essential for your religious and magical workings.

Paints and Enamels

When we discussed painting in chapter 8, we were referring to painting symbols on your ritual tool with acrylic paint. In this section we will discuss painting the entire surface of your ritual tool with enamel paint to give it a hard, water-resistant coating of paint in any specific color you desire. Enamel is a tough, durable paint. Unless you plan to paint or enamel your ritual tool, you may skip over this section.

While staining will enhance the natural pigment of your ritual tool, it will not protect it from the elements and the color choices are limited to wood tones. Finishing your ritual tool with a clear coat of varnish, shellac, or lacquer will protect your wood, whether it is stained or unstained, but a finish coat has no color or pigment in it. Enameling your tool will help protect your wood and provide you with a virtually unlimited choice of colors.

Many different kinds of paint, including enamels, are found at your local paint dealer, art supply, or craft store. Several paints are specially made for wood projects. Not only will these help preserve and protect wood, but they are also washable, durable, suitable for indoor or outdoor use, and have a dirt-resistant, shiny finish.

Enameled ritual items can only be described as unique and magical in appearance. Enameled ritual items are "workable paintings" that can be entirely painted with symbols and other creative multi-colored designs. One ceremonial magician we know wanted her staff enameled in a color that was a shade or two lighter than her purple velvet ritual robe. She took a small sample of the robe to her paint dealer who developed a perfect color. However, some pagans dislike the natural wood being painted with enamel, and claim the implement looks "graffiti-ed."

Polyurethane enamels are extremely strong and heat resistant. Water-based latex (acrylic) enamels are durable, easily applied, and easily cleaned-up. However, they are not available in a high-gloss texture.

Enamels are available in flat, gloss, and semi-gloss finishes. A flat enamel will result in a dull coloring, whereas gloss or semi-gloss will give you a shiny color.

There is a wide variety of colors available, and your paint dealer can even blend shades to match specific objects and furnishings of your sacred space. Ask for color samples to help you decide, or bring an object as a sample of the color you desire.

Enamel can be saved and stored indefinitely. Be sure to follow the instructions on the container.

Staining is not recommended at all when using enamel. The enamel color coats the wood and acts as a finish.

Enameling Your Wood

Step 1   *Preparation—applying fillers and sealers.*

If your wood has knots, pronounced creases, or any flaws, you may want to use a wood filler to even out the surface before any paint is applied. After using wood filler, apply a light sealer coat of white shellac to ensure a smooth application of the enamel.

If directions on the enamel container call for a primer or undercoat to first be applied, do so, allowing it to dry overnight, then apply your enamel.

Step 2   *Application.*

Stir the enamel gently to prevent bubbles, but let it sit thoroughly. A brush is used to apply enamel. With your brush, apply one coat with long, even strokes. Work in one direction. Brush on horizontally and turn the wood as you go along. As you paint, occasionally return to your starting point, and without applying more enamel to the brush, gently stroke back and forth to ensure that the coat is even.

Step 3   *Drying.*

When you have completed the application of a coat, lay the project in a safe area or prop it upright to dry. The enamel will set evenly. Allow this first coat to dry for twenty-four hours or longer if needed. Check to make sure that the first coat is completely dry before continuing.

Step 4   *Sanding.*

After letting the paint dry for a day, sand the project with a fine-grit sandpaper. You may need to wear eye protection and a dust mask during this process for safety. Sanding rids your project of any rough spots or uneven build-up of enamel. It also takes down shine.

Step 5 *Applying additional coats.*
If more coats of enamel are applied, sand after each coat has dried. Adequate drying time between each coat is needed. Two coats usually are sufficient, although a high-gloss shine can be obtained with a third coat.

Step 6 *Rubbing.*
You can rub the dry enamel with a clean cloth to achieve a deep gloss without excessive shine.

10

Ritual Tool Decoration

In this chapter you will find many suggestions for decorating your ritual tools, including descriptions of various symbolism that can be used for this purpose. The decorative recommendations offered here include traditional symbols of Witchcraft and other religious and magical traditions, as well as new ideas available to the contemporary pagan.

We humans often allow other people to dictate how we should conduct many aspects of our lives. We often suppress our own creativity by listening to others rather than relying on our own inspiration and experiences. The decoration of your ritual tool provides an opportunity for you to express your own creativity and personal beliefs. Once your ritual tool has been constructed, take a few moments to consider what personal symbols and decoration you would like to apply to it. Your symbols should be an expression of your individuality. The possibilities for ornamentation are endless.

Useful Materials for Decoration

- Copper wire
- Leather
- Feathers
- Jewelry
- Beads
- Semi-precious stones
- Fabric
- Ribbon
- Clear drying craft or fabric glue
- Heavy, durable scissors

Recycling Old Materials into New Decoration

Possible decorations for your ritual tools already exist right in your home. Unless you wish to use precious stones or unusual adornments, many art and craft materials can be found in your jewelry box, closet, and dresser drawers. We are firm believers in recycling—and this also applies to many old and discarded items you already own. Coupled with your creativity, these items can take on a new use as decorations for your religious and magical tools.

Jewelry

Most of us have old jewelry we no longer wear, but hold onto because it has value of some kind. These kinds of jewelry pieces are ideal for decoration. A necklace can be draped from the top of your staff or wand by gluing or screwing it onto the surface of the wood. You might consider adding pendants or charms to your ritual tool, as well. We have seen gold necklaces displaying tiny pentagrams, stars, moons, suns, and antique trinkets draped down staffs and wands. Precious stones can be carefully removed from jewelry and glued to your ritual tool.

A Wiccan friend once told us of a diamond and pearl bracelet that she owned. The piece had a broken clasp she'd never had repaired.

She removed the diamonds and pearls and attached them to her ritual knife, forming them into a gorgeous pattern.

If you have pieces of costume jewelry that you no longer wear, lay them out on a bare table and try to visualize what they would look like if they adorned your implement. A spark of creativity here can lead to a beautifully decorated tool.

Copper Wire

Copper wire is considered a wonderful addition to any ritual tool because of its unique qualities, which aid in the projection of energies. It can sometimes be found in the household garage or in the family tool chest. Copper wire and copper piping (used by plumbers) can be purchased in hardware stores and home-building centers. We suggest that you check these sources before purchasing copper wire from a New Age shop, which may charge a great deal more money. A little cleaning and reshaping of the copper is all that is needed before applying it or wrapping it onto your ritual tool.

Leather

Old leather boots, skirts, and jackets can be sources of dyed hide. This recycled leather can be wrapped around the top end of your ritual staff or the entire length of your wand, used to construct and decorate your shield, or employed to create a leather sachet for carrying your rune set. A 6" x 6" piece of leather can be glued to the top end of your ritual staff, or secured with leather thongs or copper wire, as a decorative "hand grip." Leather can be cut into strips, braided, and glued to the wood surface of your staff, wand, knife handle, or shield. You can allow the remaining ends of the braided straps to hang loosely for a festive, fringed effect. Leather strips of fringe can also be glued down the sides of your staff or wand.

To extract leather from boots, simply take a knife and carefully cut the leather beginning at the sole. Leather from old clothing can be cleaned with saddle soap or a similar product. If you do not have any old leather items, it may be possible to find some at flea markets, thrift-shops, and second-hand stores for a very modest price. There is no sense spending a lot of money on leather for your ritual tools when you might be able to obtain it for little or nothing.

Ribbon

Fabric stores carry a wide variety of ribbons in various colors and sizes. Birthday and holiday displays in department stores also offer an assortment of ribbons. Ribbons can be braided into alluring patterns around the shaft of your staff, wand, or knife handle, and glued into place. Using different colored ribbon as you braid produces a festive, colorful tool that is perfect for use in ritual dancing and celebration. Allowing many inches of the ribbon ends to hang freely, flowing like streamers through the air, can create an enchanting effect.

You may already have new or used ribbon in a sewing box, in storage, or somewhere in your home. Old lingerie often has beautiful lace and ribbon that can be recycled for the adornment of your tools.

Antlers and Bones

We recently had the opportunity to examine a ritual staff purchased by a friend at a Renaissance Fair. At the top of the sycamore staff was a three-point buck antler from a white-tailed deer. The craftsman probably attached the antler to the staff by drilling a hole into both the top end of the staff and the base of the antler. Then, using a headless screw, he secured the two pieces together. Like the wood itself, the antler was also lightly finished with a protective coating.

Deer antlers or animal bones make excellent ritual staff ornaments for practitioners of a nature religion or Shamanic tradition. You can fashion a staff similar to the one described above. You could also attach two antlers to either side of your ritual staff, and perhaps smaller antlers to your wand as well.

Feathers, Beads, and Stones

Real or synthetic feathers are easily obtained through craft stores, Native American craft shops, and many New Age bookstores. Turkey feathers, simulated eagle feathers, and peacock feathers can be very attractive additions to your ritual tools. The Shaman Rattle Staff, wand, shield, and ritual knife handle may be enhanced with leather straps knotted onto the end of feather quills. The straps can then be braided and secured so that the feathers hang freely. Beads can be added to enhance the leather straps knotted to the feather quills. Turquoise can be glued to the surface of your ritual tool to provide a

Shamanic look. It only takes your creativity and a few supplies to fashion a truly unique and enchanting ritual tool.

Semi-precious stones, pebbles, rocks, and minerals can be attached to your ritual tools with clear drying craft glue. Perhaps you already have a collection of minerals or stones that have special meaning to you. Adding these cherished natural objects to your tools can only benefit your use of them by enhancing your emotions and focusing your mind during your magical-religious practice.

Attaching Wooden Ornaments

Craft stores often sell a variety of finials, balls, crosses, and other ornaments made from pine or other soft wood. Wooden ornaments can be attached to the top of a ritual staff using a "headless screw" as follows:

MATERIALS NEEDED

- Wooden or metal ornaments
- Headless screw
- Wire cutters

Step 1 *Drilling.*
Drill a hole into both the top end of the staff and the base of the ornament.

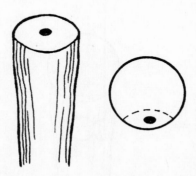

Step 1. Drill a hole into both the top end of the staff and the base of the ornament.

Step 2 *Attaching the screw.*

Insert a headless screw into the top of the staff.

Step 2. Insert a headless screw into the top of the staff through the hole you've drilled in Step 1.

Step 3 *Attaching the ornament.*

The wooden ornament can then screwed on to the headless screw which sticks out of the staff's top end.

Note: Pouring wood glue into the holes drilled into both pieces will help secure the hold. Once both pieces are attached, be sure to wipe off excess glue.

Step 3. Screw the wooden ornament on to the headless screw sticking out of the staff's top end.

Attaching Metal Ornaments

It is also possible to purchase metal ornaments from craft shops or hardware stores. For example, those practicing a Celtic tradition could secure a Celtic Cross to the butt of the knife handle or top end of the ritual staff or wand.

If the cross is made from wood, you can attach it using a headless screw as described above. If not, you will be unable to screw it onto your ritual tool. If your cross (or other ornament) is made from metal, you may attach it to your staff as follows.

Step 1   *Cutting into the staff.*

Using a sharp knife and a chisel, cut an indentation into the top end of your wooden staff the same size as the width and length of the cross's base.

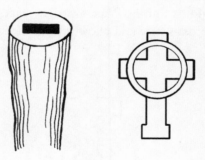

Step 1. Use a sharp knife to cut an indentation into the top end of your staff that matches the cross' base.

Step 2   *Gluing.*

Place a generous amount of wood glue in the indentation. (diagram 2, page 168)

Step 2. Place wood glue in the indentation.

Step 3 *Attaching the ornament.*
Insert the cross into the indentation that you have made. It should fit tightly. Wipe away the excess glue from around the cross's base and allow it to dry for twenty-four hours.

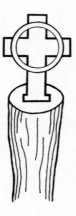

Step 3. Insert the cross into the indentation and wipe excess glue from around the base.

Step 4 *Securing.*

Once the glue has dried, you may wish to reinforce the secure hold by wrapping the base of your cross and upper part of the ritual tool shaft tightly with a leather thong.

Step 4. Secure the cross in place by wrapping the base tightly with a leather thong.

A Hand-grip for the Ritual Staff

The idea of a ritual staff hand-grip may seem unusual. However, a hand-grip is a beautiful ornament that provides a practical benefit—comfort for your hand while holding your staff during lengthy rites.

The illustration on this page shows an example of a staff with a hand-grip that we recently crafted for a friend. In creating the staff, we carved symbols into it and stained it a rich, light walnut. It was a fine looking staff, but we couldn't resist placing some ornaments on it. We purchased a cut-glass ball, about the size of a fifty-cent piece, from a home center. The cut-glass sphere was actually

Example of a hand grip for a ritual staff.

manufactured as a cabinet door handle, although it resembled a crystal ball. It had a gold-plated base with inverted threads to allow it to be screwed onto cabinet doors. We found a "headless screw" which we inserted into the staff's top end and screwed the glass ball onto it. Next, we cut a 5″ x 5″ square from an old red suede skirt. To attach this leather piece to the top end of the staff, we applied non-toxic clear-drying craft glue to the wood surface. Then, we carefully wrapped the leather tightly to the top of the staff, forming a decorative hand-grip. With plenty of leather straps wrapped around the leather hand-grip, we tied a knot around the top of the hand-grip and wrapped the strap around it until it reached the bottom, where we tied another knot. The leather strap was not only decorative, it firmly held the leather in place for the glue to dry. Using purple satin fabric, we sewed together a tiny purse with a draw string. Inside the purse we placed mugwort, an herb that our friend often uses in ritual. The purse was also tied around the leather hand-grip, and we wove its purple strings through the leather strap before the final knotting.

Embroidering the Hand-grip

When designing a hand-grip you may wish to take a piece of plain, colored fabric and embroider a symbol or two on it with colored thread. If you have not attempted embroidery before, give it a try—you do not need to be an expert in needlework to do it. We have found that preparation and patience yields the best results. Draw your symbols on the fabric in pencil first. This will give you a guide to follow as you embroider.

A hand-grip can be of any fabric, leather, or fleece; and the choice of your material is another symbol of your magical-spiritual practice. Ornaments chosen for your ritual tool decoration reflect what pleases your sensibilities and how you practice your beliefs. A black satin hand-grip with an embroidered white, upright pentagram in the center will imply that you are well-versed in the magical arts of witchcraft. A green cotton fabric with shamrocks or the Celtic cross will indicate that you practice a Celtic religion.

Adding a Crystal to your Wand or Staff

A crystal can be an attractive addition to any ritual tool. Placing a stone or crystal on the top end of a staff or wand or at the bottom end of a knife handle is not very difficult. We recommend using a crystal or stone that is no more than two inches in diameter—if the crystal is any larger than this, it might be difficult to secure it to your implement. It may also look odd if the stone were larger than the diameter of your tool. Oblong crystals are the best choice.

Materials Needed

- Oblong crystal (2" or less in diameter)
- Thin wire
- Thick wire (clothes hanger thickness)
- Heavy scissors or wire cutters
- Clear-drying craft glue
- Knife
- Yarn or leather strips (optional)

Step 1   *Secure the crystal into place.*
A simple way to secure the crystal or stone is by first wrapping it with wire. While any type of wire will work, wire used in jewelry-making or copper wire is ideal. At least half of the crystal should be tightly wrapped in the wire brace.

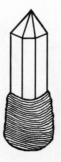

Step 1. Wrap your crystal with wire. At least half of the crystal should be tightly wrapped.

Step 2   *Gluing.*

Next, apply clear-drying craft glue generously to the wire brace around the bottom of the crystal. Allow the glue to dry thoroughly.

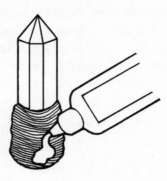

Step 2. Apply clear-drying craft glue to the wire brace around the bottom of your crystal.

Step 3   *Cutting thicker wire.*

Cut four pieces of thick wire, each 2" long. One inch of the thick wire will be used to brace the stone and the other inch will lay against the staff.

Step 4   *Cutting the grooves.*

With a knife, carve four grooves, each an inch long, into the wood surface at the top of your ritual tool.

Step 4. Carve four 1" grooves into the wood surface at the top of your ritual tool.

Step 5 *Attaching and gluing.*

Place the four pieces of thick wire inside these grooves and glue them into place.

Step 5. Place one piece of wire into each of the four grooves and glue them into place.

Step 6 *Final Wrapping.*

Insert the bottom of crystal between the four thick wires. Using the thin wire, wrap around the thicker wire brace it is completely covered. Try to wind the thin wire in neat circles around the staff. Remember to leave the top half of your crystal or stone uncovered so that it is visible. Apply glue to any gaps where the wire circles the wood.

Step 7 *Optional finishing steps.*

If you do not like the wire showing, you can braid ribbon or wind colored yarn or leather around it. (diagram 7, page 174).

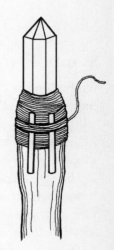

Step 6. Insert the crystal between the four wires and wrap wire around the brace.

Step 7. If you choose, you can braid ribbon around the wire base for a more decorative look.

◆ ◆ ◆

Symbols

Symbolism has been used in spiritual and magical practices for thousands of years. This may be due to the fact that every spell or magical working is a ritual manipulation of symbols. Whether or not religions claim to practice magic, symbols play an important role in religious worship.

The application of symbols on ritual tools, personal belongings, and as ornaments to adorn sacred space, brings an awareness of the underlying principles and worship and magic that allows for connection with deity or ritual manipulation of the symbol and what it represents.

There is an endless array of symbols that can be used in the decoration of ritual items. The symbols that appear in this book are defined according to the most common interpretations and uses in contemporary religious and magical practices. In some cases, the historical use of a particular symbol is not known and the same symbol may be used by different people who impart unique meanings to it.

It is important that you familiarize yourself with the most common meanings of your chosen symbols, but you must use them in a manner that you feel is appropriate.

One person's interpretation of a symbol may not be that of another. For example, one of our clients requested that we paint the Crusader's Cross on his ritual knife because he felt the cross was a protective symbol and a symbol of victory in all quests—whether physical, mental, or spiritual. His interpretation of this symbol may be different from that of someone else. Therefore, studying the definition of a commonly used symbol is ideal, but you must interpret a symbol for its key use and purpose as it relates to you. Symbols are an intimate part of an individual's life and beliefs.

The work we have accomplished in making ritual tools for others has provided us the opportunity to study various religious and magical symbols. Each individual request has taught us about both ancient and contemporary religious or magical practice, as well as allowed us the challenge of applying symbols we had not used before.

There are many techniques for applying symbolism to ritual tools. Here we will examine several application methods, as well as various symbols from which you may choose or perhaps develop ideas of your own.

Carving, Wood Branding, and Painting Your Symbols

The bulk of the instruction on how to carry out these techniques are given in chapter 8. In this section, we provide some illustrations and photographs of different wood carvings, paintings, and wood brandings that you may choose to recreate for your own ritual tools. The application of your personal spiritual symbolism should be regarded as a very sacred and magical act. As you carve, paint, or brand your implement, you are infusing the tool with energies of your inner self, or "inner power." This process is a ritual in itself, and one that is quite enjoyable.

Your first attempt at the application of symbolism to your implement might be your symbols, your pagan name, a personal expression written in a magical alphabet, or whatever design you choose. The following pages show examples of symbols that we have applied to various wooden ritual tools. We have defined symbols in terms of its ease of reproduction—whether it is a simple, intermediate, or complex symbol—along with the easiest approach to applying each symbol. If your desired symbols are not shown in this book, find those that are most similar and follow the suggested guidelines for application.

Painting and wood branding are the simplest techniques for beginners. Both methods allow for easy application and mistakes are quickly erased with sand paper. Painting allows you to use a variety of colors, and some feel it is the most simple technique.

For the best results in painting, practice your designs on paper first. Then draw your symbols on your ritual tool with a pencil. Whatever technique you use, apply your symbols carefully and take your time.

Carving any symbol, whether it is circular or straight-lined, will be a challenge depending upon the wood grain of your chosen wood. For instance, pine is difficult to carve; its wood grain flakes and results in straight lines that never appear perfectly straight unless the carving is extremely deep. On the other hand, poplar is very easy to carve because its wood grain does not flake.

Simple Symbols

Runes

Runes are an alphabet as well as a system of symbols for divination and magic. They are simple designs that can be applied to your implement by carving, painting, or wood branding. Examples of these symbols are given in chapter 6.

Single runes used for the sole purpose of symbolism often reflect strengths or abilities (such as courage), that you wish to acquire. In runescript, the magician lines up a group of runes in such a way that, if he or she found them so associated in a runecast, they would fore-shadow or predict the very event desired.[1] If the magician felt satis-fied that this runecast faithfully reproduced the situation that was desired, the next step would be to write the symbols out on a clean slip of white paper, or carve it onto wood or a piece of metal.[2]

Select an method from chapter 8 to apply these to your tool. Fol-lowing the outlined steps regarding application, proceed with patience and a gentle hand. If you chose to carve runes onto your staff, wand, or knife handle, a light stain should be applied to enhance the symbols and make them more visible on the wood's surface.

Astrological Signs

The zodiacal symbols are used frequently by astrologers and others practicing certain forms of magic. The definitions and magical properties of the zodiacal symbols are extensive; at times the properties differ from one system of divination or magic to another. For this reason we list them below, without definition, for your reference.

Planetary symbols and zodiacal signs are rather simple to apply. No matter what procedure you choose to apply these symbols, you

≈	Aquarius	♓	Pisces
♈	Aries	♉	Taurus
♊	Gemini	♋	Cancer
♌	Leo	♍	Virgo
♎	Libra	♏	Scorpio
♐	Sagittarius	♑	Capricorn
♅	Uranus	⊕	Earth
☽	Moon	♃	Jupiter
☿	Mercury	♄	Saturn
♇	Pluto	♆	Neptune
♀	Vulcan		

Astrological Symbols.

might want to draw them first in pencil on your tool, then begin your technique of application slowly. The pencil drawing helps provide you with a pattern to follow, and it can be easily erased if a mistake is made.

Crosses

The Egyptian Ankh, Celtic Cross, Christian Cross, and Russian Orthodox Cross (three-bar cross) are all very simple designs. An example of each is shown below.

When carving any type of cross, take a small folded piece of sand paper and carefully sand inside the grooves of each carving. This will help you attain a smooth and pronounced cross carving.

Crosses (from left to right): Egyptian Ankh, Celtic Cross, Christian Cross, Russian Orthodox Cross.

Intermediate Symbols

A symbol with a swirling or circular pattern, flower designs, or facial features, such as faces drawn upon images of the Sun or Moon, are considered intermediate, as are certain magical alphabets. Perhaps your spiritual or magical path uses such an alphabet. Any writing containing curves and intricate patterns fit into this category. Actually, the application of alphabets is as easy as writing on paper; however, the wood grain will present a degree of resistance to curves, and applying the letters or words evenly next to one another, or in a straight line, can be frustrating. To avoid such frustration, draw your letters or words in pencil on the wood before you begin.

Alphabets

If you practice a Celtic religion, you will be relieved to know that the Ogham Alphabet (above) is extremely simple to carve, wood brand, or paint. This alphabet is a system of writing employed by the Druids, and in ancient eras it was known as Boibel-Loth, or "Tree Writing."[3] A whole system of magic sprang from this Tree Alphabet, primarily within the Celtic religious traditions.[4] The Ogham Alphabet consists of letters symbolized by straight lines or marks. Some of the marks slant slightly, but do not pose much difficulty to the beginner. This particular alphabet works especially well for wood branding. We have also included the Theban alphabet, which appears on page 180.

If you are interested in applying symbols of a magical alphabet to your ritual tool, but do not have a good source of symbols to refer to, Raymond Buckland's *Buckland's Complete Book of Witchcraft* (Llewellyn Publications), offers an extensive display of illustrated magical alphabets, along with their historical and contemporary use. There is really no set guideline for carving or wood branding these alphabets. Practice is the best teacher.

A   B   C   D   E   F

G   H   I   J   M   N

Ng   O   P   Q   R   S

T   U   V

The Ogham Alphabet.

A	B	C	D	E	F

G	H	I	K	L	M

N	O	P	Q	R	S

T	V	X	Y	Z	

The Theban Alphabet.

We have never avoided the application of any design simply because someone told us it was too difficult to reproduce. If you want to apply a particular symbol to your implement, give it try, no matter how detailed or intricate the design is. The key is to carve or wood brand lightly and carefully at first—allowing mistakes to be sanded away before carving or branding deeply into the wood surface.

Before carving an intermediate design on your ritual tool, practice on scrap wood. It may take several attempts before you are comfortable with the technique of carving.

Complex Symbols

People, detailed figures of Gods and Goddesses, dragons, fairies, pentagrams, animals, and any design with extensive detail is considered complex.

Figures, Animals, and Geometric Designs

Some might find it odd that we place the pentagram in this category. The pentagram is a mathematically designed symbol—if you desire a perfect, equal-armed five-pointed star, then you are in for some geometry! Never attempt to carve or brand a pentagram without first measuring it out on the wood surface with either a compass or ruler. Not only are the line lengths measured, but also the space between the center pentagon and the interior of each of the five triangular arms.

Whether or not you are artistically inclined, you can work with any of the three categories of symbolism (simple, intermediate, and complex) listed above. Take a moment to consider the wooden figures and carvings of the ancients; some are intricately detailed and appear as if they were time consuming and extremely difficult to produce. Other archaic carvings appear as if a child had whittled away at the wood with a knife. The amount of detail your personal symbolism contains is not important. What is important is that you are satisfied with how the symbol looks.

You are your own judge and worst critic in this process. As you apply a symbol to your ritual tool, you will notice every single variation of the symbol's design. Ask a friend to comment on your work before judging it yourself; you may be too critical.

The decoration of your ritual tools can be as limited or extensive as you would like. We once examined a staff that was custom-made for an astrologer. All the signs of the zodiac were carved on one side of the staff. Along the other side were her personal symbols: the pentagram, the Wiccan Triple Goddess symbol (two crescent moons on either side of the full moon), the symbol of her own zodiacal sign, and her pagan name of "Mooncatcher Soothsayer" in the Theban magical alphabet. This particular staff contained great amount of complex symbolism. Carving the zodiac signs, each symbolized by a mythic creature, is extremely intricate and challenging.

Another example of a ritual tool with complex symbolism was an oak staff we recently crafted for a practitioner of the Celtic religion. The symbolism on the staff consisted of a painting of the face of the Celtic God known as the "Green Man," who embodies the two-fold concept of life following death, while emphasizing the creative power of ancient Celtic Tree Magic.[5] This staff was considered by Celtic lore as "the oak club." (It also appears in the form of a staff or spear similar to St. George's lance and the judgment stick of the Egyptian God Anubis.[6])

To paint the Green Man onto the staff, we used forest green paint to display colorful foliage around the Green Man's face, outlining and enhancing the vein structure of each leaf in a darker green. The eyes, nose, and mouth were painted in a greenish-black color. The owner of the staff specified that a maroon Celtic Cross outlined in pale yellow be painted beneath the Green Man. We wood branded the practitioner's Celtic name, along with the phrase "the King of Light and the Dark Tannest," (titles of the Green Man), in the Ogham alphabet in a circle at the center of the staff. The remaining area, extending to the bottom end of the staff, was painted with circles of red, orange, yellow, green, blue, indigo, and violet, representing the colors of the chakras. The chakras are energy centers that, according to Eastern mysticism, exist within the human body. The names of the chakras—Muladhara, Svadisthana, Manipura, Anahata, Vishuddu, Ajna, and Sahasrara—were painted on the staff in the correct colors.

When finished, the unstained staff was lightly sprayed with a protective clear coat. We completed the staff by tying a red leather handgrip to its top end, securing it with leather straps, and cutting a groove in the staff's top end for insertion of a brass Celtic Cross, which was carefully glued into place. Strings of tiny brass bells were looped around the Celtic Cross and down the hand-grip, where they cascaded down the upper half of the staff. The decoration of this particular staff indicates that its owner employs it for both magical work and Celtic devotional rites.

Examples of Ritual Tool Decoration

Among all the staffs and wands that we have created for individuals over the years, we consider those of Native American and shamanic traditions to be some of the most earthy and beautiful. One of our favorite designs is that of a snake carved around the shaft of a wand or staff, which symbolizes the constant flowing and spiraling movement of the transformational energy that turns the spiritual into the material.[7] An example of this is shown on the cover of this book.

A carved snake may have a crystal placed in its mouth, to indicate the staff's potential in focusing and directing radiant energy.[8] The crystal is also believed to hold and balance the energy that is infused into it. Bells and feathers are often applied to the staff to create a gentle sound when the implement is shaken. Symbols appropriate to the individual shaman are carved and painted onto the shaft and sometimes on the bottom end of the staff.[9]

We once designed and crafted an athame that was to be used by an older woman who followed the teachings of Gerald Gardner, the founder of the Gardnerian tradition of Wicca. The athame is a tool primarily designed for individual use; it is not to be used by the entire coven. The woman wanted to use the athame for the purpose of directing power in ritual and in spell casting. We were commissioned to construct the athame, paint its wooden handle black, and add symbols taken from *The Key of Solomon*, a classic magical text dating from the sixteenth century. The symbols were to be divided into two sections, one on each side of the knife's handle, as depicted in MacGregor Mathers' translation of *The Key of Solomon* and Gardner's *Book of Shadows*.

For the knife handle's construction, we followed the same procedures outlined in Chapter 5. We used acrylic paint—black for the handle and assorted colors for the symbols. A protective coat was sprayed on the finished knife handle to ensure a lifetime of use. At our client's request, we did not photograph this athame. However, with the woman's kind permission, we have listed the symbols painted on her athame below, along with their meanings and illustrations. You may or may not find a similarity between these symbols and those that you choose to adorn your own tools. This demonstrates the sacred and personal meaning of ritual tools and symbols chosen by each individual for their spiritual practices.

First side of the athame handle:

Horned God

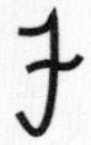

Initial of His Name

Kiss and Scourge

Waxing and Waning Moon

Initials of several Goddess names in Hebrew script

Second side of the athame handle:

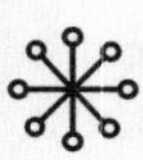

Eight Ritual Occasions, Eight Weapons, etc.

The Sickle; a symbol of Death

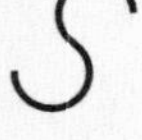

The Serpent; a symbol of Life and Rebirth

Another interesting example is an athame we created for a Third Degree High Priestess. She and her High Priest had successfully run a coven for ten years. The High Priest called upon us to construct an athame for her, adorned with the following symbols:

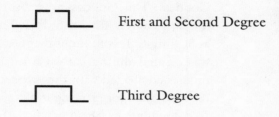

First and Second Degree

Third Degree

Note that the first symbol is different than the second; it has a space in the center. This is to symbolize the High Priest and Priestess working together through the First and Second Degree initiations as man and woman; the masculine and feminine aspects of nature in the philosophy of witchcraft. The last symbol indicates their perfect union after completion of a third degree initiation. It represents the kneeling man and kneeling woman now united together in perfect spiritual marriage within their coven.

Symbolism on a ritual tool can be as unique as the individual who creates it. No two ritual items that we have created have ever been identical.

In applying symbols to ritual tools created for our clients, we have often wondered about the intent of the individual. Many people request the application of a great deal of seemingly unrelated symbolism to their implements. Trying to decipher the purpose of this is like trying to fit pieces of a puzzle together. Below are a few symbols which we have applied to ritual tools—separately or in conjunction with other symbols. These may provide you with ideas if you are not sure what symbols use in the decoration of your personal tools.

Selected Symbolism for Ritual Tools

Bridget's Cross

Symbolic of the Celtic Goddess, Brigid, this emblem represents her aspect of fertility, as well as her role as the triple Muse-Goddess. This Goddess was absorbed by the early church; Christians recognized her as St. Brigid. It is thought that her symbol was created during early Christian ceremonies connected with the preparation of the seed grain for growing in the spring.[15] In contemporary pagan practice, the cross represents the sacred preservation of the highest wisdom by the organization of both community and solitary religious observations.[16] In either case, it is clearly evident that the cross represents religious ritual.

The Crusaders Cross

This cross is sometimes called the Jerusalem Cross. It represents the eternal motion of life, with the equilateral crosses each symbolizing wheels of life within the greater wheel of the Universe.[17]

Drop of Blood

Blood symbolizes the fluid that carries the life-force. In some religions and magical traditions, it is thought that a drop of blood carries the individual's life-force within it. This symbol can be applied to a magician's wand and used for positive practice, not manipulation or destruction.

The Eye of Horus

This is an Egyptian symbol that represents ceremonies and rituals that involve using and obtaining sacred wisdom. The Eye of Horus can be considered a symbol of protection which guards both sacred knowledge and the workings of magicians. It is often applied to magician's tools.

Lotus Blossom

This symbol represents the multiple aspects of Self, blossoming within the highest realm of spirit. Often, the chakras are applied somewhere on a ritual tool with the lotus blossom depicting the crown chakra. The lotus blossom indicates the individual awakening and expanding in consciousness to charter the spiritual realm, resulting in personal growth.[10]

The Maltese Cross

This cross is often requested by magicians. It emphasizes the action of energy flowing out from the center in a direct, balanced manner.[12] At times, the cross's four arms are used to symbolize the four elements.

The Pillar

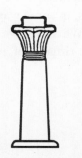

This is frequently used on ritual tools that assist the owner in entering the world of the psyche. In the tarot card of the High Priestess, two pillars are shown; one white and one black. The black pillar is the feminine and unconscious side of the mind, while the white pillar represents masculine and the material world.[13] Walking between the two pillars takes you into the realm of the psyche.

The Pyramid

This is a symbol used by a broad spectrum of religious and magical practitioners. It represents directing energy to the realms beyond and receiving divine energy from the spiritual realm. It symbolizes the sacred, etheric forces which transmit all energies to and from the spiritual realm.[14]

The Spoked Wheel

This represents the Wheel of Life as it turns the cycles of life; the seasons, birth, death, and rebirth. Many pagan religions that actively work with the cycles of life and self-transformation use this symbol to represent harmony with nature, and the natural forces and cycles of the universe. The turning of the Wheel indicates spiritual evolution.

The Temple

This symbol represents the holy place within the self where our personal connection to spirit is honored.[11] It is interesting to note that the Temple is often referred to as "the house." The symbol is the same yet the house represents, in some way, the properties of a healer. (Whenever we have applied this symbol to a ritual tool, it was usually for a healer.)

The Elements

There are countless symbols that are used to depict the four elements of nature. Since many religious and magical traditions revere or magically harness the energies of the elements, such symbols are frequently placed on ritual tools, and upon the appropriate candles.

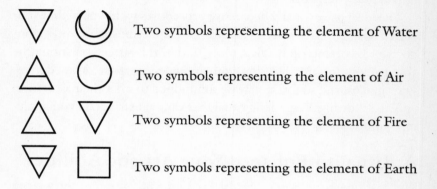

Two symbols representing the element of Water

Two symbols representing the element of Air

Two symbols representing the element of Fire

Two symbols representing the element of Earth

Choosing Your Symbols

We have listed some frequently used symbols in this chapter to assist you in determining which emblems might best work for you and may be applied to your ritual tool. There are certainly many symbols of various religious and magical origin that are not listed here. If you would like additional information on symbols, a few source books are listed in the Suggested Reading section of this book.

Keep in mind that your choice of symbols has much to do with your ritual tool's primary function. Will the tool be used only for devotional rites, or only for magic? Will you use your tool for both? Is your tool mainly dedicated to healing, like the medicine shield, or is it primarily a tool for the invocation of your deities? These questions will help you decide what symbolism to use. You can apply symbols of both a religious and a magical nature upon your implement if it is to be used for both purposes. On the other hand, you may wish to apply only those symbols which represent your deity and reflect your religion.

A magician may choose the Eye of Horus, symbols of the four elements, runescripts, a pentagram, and personal sigils. A Celtic religious practitioner may choose to employ the Celtic Cross, Brigid's Cross, his or her pagan name, or a phrase written in the Ogham alphabet.

Once you have established what symbols you intend to use, you must decide what technique you will use to apply them, collect the tools and materials for their application, and schedule a suitable time to conduct your work.

The ideal place for any decorative procedures would be within your sacred space, this is where you will find the atmosphere most conducive to working on magical tools, and in this space you should be able to concentrate solely on your intended purpose. Your deities, spirit guides, and so forth, may be summoned to offer their assistance.

The following is a generic ritual that can be used to aid you applying symbolism to your ritual tool.

A Ritual to Enhance Your Artistic Abilities

The best time to perform this ritual is on the full moon or the waxing moon. The waxing moon is beneficial for the practice of constructive magic. It will help you in positive ventures. The time of day or night is unimportant, but you need to be free from distractions, such as the telephone, and the everyday hustle and bustle of humanity.

For this ceremony, it is best if your ritual tool is not fully decorated with bells, ribbon, top ornaments, a hand-grip, or other secondary decorations that may get in your way or distract your concentration. You may wish to add these adornments during the ritual, after you apply your primary symbolism.

Any of the these locations—your sacred space, a personal altar set up somewhere in your home, or an area outside the home that allows you privacy—are ideal places in which to perform the ritual given below. You will need only your ritual implement and the tools and materials needed to apply your desired symbolism. Bring a pencil and a couple of sheets of white paper to practice drawing your symbols first. The pencil will also be used to draw your symbols on your ritual tool as a pattern. If you are carving or wood branding, take a scrap piece of sand paper to erase possible errors. If you are painting, bring brushes, paints, and a cup of water to clean your brushes (bring turpentine for oil-based paints).

If you do not have a designated sacred space, then any area offering you privacy and quiet is suitable.

There is no need to change your clothing or to feel obligated to wear ritual garb for this occasion. If you are carving, painting, or wood branding, you will not want to risk staining or damaging formal ritual clothing.

If your religious or magical path performs a circle casting or similar rite, you may wish to conduct it beforehand, although it is not necessary to do so. The focus and goal of this ritual is to allow communion with your deities, spirit guides, guardian angel, or the divine source of your choice for the purpose of providing you guidance and inspiration during this artistic endeavor.

Once you are inside your designated sacred space, sit down in a comfortable position and place your ritual tool, hand tools, and other materials on the ground next to you. Take a moment to relax and meditate. Clear your consciousness and visualize a golden light surrounding you, your ritual tool, and your other tools. The golden light surrounding you should feel warm and secure; its purpose is to purify your sacred space, clear your conscious mind of clutter, and initiate communion between you and your divine source. Do not use your physical senses, such as sight or hearing, for this exercise. Use your mind's eye to visualize the golden light and absorb your psyche in its presence.

As the golden light is absorbed into your mind and body, inhale slowly and gently through your nose, and exhale slowly through your mouth to help you relax. Breathe in this fashion four times in a row, pausing between each breath by saying "one." (Some individuals say "OM," others say "down." These words are mantras that help to focus the mind and pull the spirit plane down to the physical plane.)

When you feel at peace, both physically and mentally, call upon your divine source or spirit guide to descend upon the physical plane to assist you. You may call aloud or mentally. You may visualize your divine source approaching where you are seated as you invoke, or you may simply feel its presence in your mind. There is no one correct way of conducting this union. Whatever technique is used to allow you to sense the divine presence is correct one for you.

With your eyes still closed in visualization, let go of the golden light or your source's manifestation. Now envision the symbols you wish to apply to your ritual tool. As you mentally examine each symbol, carefully note its every intricate detail. Your invoked deity or spirit guide will take note of them as well. State your intentions to your invoked guide and ask for its assistance. Describe how you will attempt to apply the symbols to your ritual tool.

Once you are certain your guide has received and reviewed your visionary messages, it is time to proceed.

Next, open your eyes and take up the pencil and sheet of paper. Have your symbol or symbols clearly defined within your mind. Draw the symbol(s)—do not rush or become frustrated if it is not perfect. Listen to the guidance of your invoked source, use the eraser or a new sheet of paper, and start again. You will succeed.

Upon completion, your divine source may suggest a different order for the symbols or even the deletion of a symbol. This may sound odd, but it has happened to us. Give your guide the benefit of the doubt, erase your work, and draw the symbols as suggested. Trust your divine source and remember that it is guiding you with utmost wisdom.

Complete each symbol until you are pleased with the final outcome. Then repeat the same procedure again, but this time draw each symbol upon your ritual tool. Doing so requires much more patience and gentleness; the wood surface will not be perfectly smooth, regardless of whether or not you sanded it beforehand. Erase errors if they occur and begin again.

After every symbol is drawn upon the ritual tool and you are pleased with the result, you are ready to begin your chosen technique of application. Speak to your guide for assistance as you work. Proceed carefully, erase if necessary with sandpaper, and above all, take pleasure from the experience. Think of what each symbol means to you, your chosen path, and your evolution in the spiritual and magical realms. Picture each symbol in your mind as if it were already completed and gracing the sacred wood of your ritual tool. In doing so, you are conducting a form of magic—you are working the spell. Visualize it completed and so shall it be!

If you cannot complete a particular design in the wood surface for some reason, state the problem to your invoked guide. Listen mentally for advice in return. If you cannot finish the application of every symbol for any reason, close your circle and end the session. Wait for the next appropriate day or time and advise your invoked guide accordingly. Remember that Rome was not built in a day—if you become tired, frustrated, or are interrupted, try again some other time.

Before closing, put all your tools down and sit once again in a relaxed, comfortable position with your eyes closed. Give your guide thanks, if not reverence, for its assistance. You may wish to expound upon the many uses that your completed ritual tool will serve, or how pleased you are with the symbols which adorn it. Give personal expression to your communion with the divine source—after all, it came to your service unconditionally.

When the time is right, and you feel the communion has ceased, collect your tools and ritual implement and close down the circle. With your ritual tool newly christened with your sacred marks, you can apply all remaining decoration at a later time. The tool's final dedication, consecration, and use within your spiritual and magical realm is close at hand.

Endnotes

1. Willis, *The Runic Workbook*, 132.
2. Ibid., 133.
3. Murray Hope. *Practical Celtic Magic* (London: The Aquarian Press, 1987), 130.
4. Ibid., 130.
5. Ibid., 173.
6. Ibid., 174.
7. Meadows, *Shamanic Experience*, 65.
8. Ibid., 65-66.
9. Ibid., 66.
10. Wolfe, *Personal Alchemy* (St. Paul: Llewellyn, 1993), 356.
11. Ibid., 356.
12. Ibid., 67.

13. Alexandra Collins Dickerman. *Following Your Path*, (Los Angeles: Jeremy P. Tarcher, Inc.), 30.
14. Wolfe, 378.
15. Janet and Stewart Farrar. *Witches Bible Compleat*, 62.
16. Wolfe, 414.
17. Ibid., 68.

11

Ritual Tool Meditation and Consecration

Since ancient times, meditation has been used in spiritual and magical practices. It is an essential tool in the awakening of the inner self, the senses, and in the evolution of the unconscious mind toward spiritual growth.

Ancient shamans and wise men and women used various meditative techniques to provide focus for the conscious mind, which for some individuals acts like a spoiled child demanding full attention at all times. These techniques included the use of hallucinogens, incense, self-hypnosis, and various tricks to keep the conscious mind busy or forcibly at rest while the unconscious mind expands its awareness for the purpose of deep meditation and communion with the worlds beyond our physical plane.

In contemporary pagan practices there are several innovative techniques that allow the conscious mind to be pacified, permitting the Higher Self and the subconscious mind time to explore the spiritual realms. Drugs and trials of self-inflicted pain are no longer necessary to obtain this goal. Once again your ritual tools can play an important role in assisting you through this growth process. When used in meditation, each ritual implement can be the projector of wisdom and provide teachings of its own.

Bonding With Your Tool

Many pagans consider their ritual tools as an extension of their physical and spiritual bodies. When a specific tool accompanies them through countless rituals and meditations, a bond is formed. The fact that the ritual staff, for example, can sustain one's balance during physical movement and offer a focal point for higher awareness, indicates the possibility of such a bond. Whichever implement you choose to work with primarily will become a part of you. The bond is formed.

Sometimes it is difficult to find the time you need to form this bond with your ritual tools. Setting aside time to plan a meditation exercise to help form this bond is important, as creating this bond offers the same relationship between master and tool as that of a psychic and his or her tarot deck, or a magician and his or her wand. Repeated use of the tarot by the psychic, in meditation and divination, establishes a bond that makes it easier for the psychic to access the spiritual realms when reading and working with the cards. The meanings and symbols of the tarot cards become second nature to the psychic, and the deck becomes an extension of the reader's psychic senses. Intimate use and insight can only benefit the reader and perpetuate the growth of the bond as the deck becomes a tool of mental extension. The same could be said of your own ritual tools once you bond and work with them.

Meditation

The meditations described in this chapter are very basic and do not require previous experience with meditation. The two exercises given in the following pages will help you get acquainted with and form a working bond with your ritual tool.

In many pagan religions, ritual meditation follows the invocation of both the elements and certain deities. Meditation allows the practitioner to calm the mind and body in preparation for ritual workings. In performing the exercises suggested here, you may choose to conduct a ritual consisting solely of meditation work. You may also choose to conduct these meditation exercises outside of your spiritual and magical circle. The decision is entirely your own.

If you are working within a group, it may be easier if one person leads the group in a meditation or narrated meditation. The first meditation discussed below emphasizes solitary meditation, while the latter one focuses on a group meditation. They are interchangeable, however, and can be altered to suit your personal needs.

Meditation for bonding with your new ritual tool is essential for awakening the psychic senses which allow the free-flowing of energies to increase when you are working with your implements. A ritual tool made of wood carries vital energies of the tree that once gave life to its wood. Meditation exercises will ensure the bonding of your personal energies with those of your wood. If your wood is strong, healthy, and rich in pigment, then rest assured that it still contains the tree's vital life-force energies within.

Visualization

A primary component of meditation is visualization. This is performed by creating a mental picture of an object, person, place, or situation. Day dreaming is a process of visualization. It is one of the techniques used in the meditation exercises given in this book.

Many people shy away from the practice of meditation. They feel their schedules are too hectic, or they can't find a time or place where they won't be interrupted. While some meditations are lengthy or require complicated technique, the meditations herein are very simple, effective, and enjoyable.

Many people find visualization difficult. They may try too hard or expect to physically see things three-dimensionally and in sharp detail. Remember that the right side of the human brain, which is the center for intuition and creativity, is not generally exercised or used as much as the left side of the brain, which is our main conductor of mental activity. If you have trouble visualizing, simply follow the meditation instructions to the best of your ability, even if you find the process difficult. There is no way you can fail in these exercises, and you should not be concerned with the clarity or "reality" of your visions.

Once you begin working with your implements, you will want to explore what wisdom lies within its wood and how you may tap into the teachings that the ritual tool has to communicate to you. Your tool's wood carries sacred messages from nature and the cosmic forces—perhaps even knowledge from our own collective subconscious, higher self.

The energies of your wooden ritual tools can deliver images that transmit divine messages into a form you can understand. This allows for the process of bonding and an intricate working relationship to develop between you and your implement.

Each tool has its own unique properties and wisdom to communicate. Exploring the energies of each one will open up channels of discovery in consciousness that will reflect your inquisitive inner self.

The following simple meditation is designed to initiate bonding with your tool. It uses the physical characteristics and qualities of the tool itself to conjure wisdom-filled messages and images. This exercise may be performed either physically, or by mental imagery alone. Both methods offer the same beneficial effects.

Bonding Meditation Exercise

It is important that you have a quiet area where you will be free from interruption during this exercise. Take the telephone off the receiver, turn off noisy appliances, and be certain you have privacy. You may choose to conduct this procedure within your sacred space or in the comfort of a quiet room in your home. A peaceful spot outdoors is fine, as well.

Choose one of the tools you have created to perform the bonding exercise. No other items are required for this process, though you may wish to have a notebook and pen handy to jot down any revealing findings or to simply record the experience for later reflection. Incense, a tape player and some New Age music, or whatever additional aids you require to obtain a meditative state of mind can also be used.

There is no right or wrong way to position your body during this meditation—many books on meditation suggest positions that are not comfortable or practical for beginners. Simply sit, lie down, or assume whatever position is most comfortable for you. If you feel well and relaxed, any position you choose is right for this exercise.

Once you are comfortable and ready, surround yourself, your ritual tool, and the immediate area with a golden or white light. This is a ritual act of purification that will help open the subconscious mind toward spiritual expansion through visualization.

As you focus on the light surrounding you, slowly direct your attention to your breathing. Relaxation through concentrated breathing is a powerful method for acquiring the receptive state of mind needed to obtain effective results. Focus on this aspect of your body; concentrate on breathing in and out. With each breath, feel your body cleansed by the pure atmosphere of nature. Feel the breathing out of stress and tension. Continue this pattern for a few breaths.

Begin rhythmic breathing; this is another technique that enhances relaxation and the calming of your consciousness. Begin as you did before, only this time inhale slowly to a count of four and exhale slowly to a count of four. Between each count of four, you may desire to say one word—a mantra that focuses your thoughts, such as "OM," "down," or "one." Perhaps your own name, or your deity's name could be used in this fashion. Repeat this procedure until a rhythmic sequence is established and you begin to feel the muscles of your body release their physical tension. As you continue, progressively let go of the visual image of golden or white light until you are fully relaxed, both mentally and physically. Your mind should be clear; no longer focused on anything.

Other relaxation techniques may also be used. Some individuals imagine a warm wave of energy gently rising from their toes to the top of their head, while others tense and relax each muscle group of the body. Perhaps you have your own method of relaxation. If so, feel free to incorporate it into this exercise.

Whether you are lying down, sitting, or standing, take your ritual tool into both hands. (If you are sitting, cup the tool in both hands and rest it on your lap. Don't tense your muscles more than is necessary to hold the tool. If lying down, rest the tool upon your chest if need be.)

Clear your mind of worries and thoughts. Inhale slowly, relax, and envision yourself venturing into that mystical place within your mind where there are no fears, worries, interference, or judgments from others. Allow yourself to become absorbed within the caverns of your mind. Forget the hectic modern world outside. At this moment, time stops for you.

Feel your ritual tool physically cupped in your hands. Allow your fingertips to caress its form, to investigate its texture. Think of nothing. Whatever images come to mind, examine them. Just because they might not seem relevant does not mean that they are not important.

Imagine that time has halted and the world around you is temporarily invisible. The only things in existence at this point are you and your tool. Calmly and without fear ask the energies within the tool if you may intrude upon their solitude in order to extract wisdom and reach new horizons of learning. You will be welcomed—as if entering the abode of old friends.

Attempt to visualize the tool within your mind's eye. Visualize it exactly as constructed. Ask yourself how its structure and decoration reflect you and your inner self.

Describe why you chose the tool's shape, color, and physical attributes, then state how the decorations reflect your beliefs and practices. Look deep within yourself to find the answers. Answer aloud or in your thoughts.

Next ask what inner wisdom the wood holds from its years of life as a branch of its mother tree. Feel the tool's wood with your fingers. Does it feel warm or cold? Dry or damp? Do you feel a smooth wood surface, or a textured one? What do you sense from the wood's energies and the completed form of the tool? Do you hear sounds or voices when concentrating upon the tool's inner energies? Do you smell the rustic woodlands from which the wood came? Breathe deeply, and contemplate slowly. Do not rush. Every question, your every thought and consideration, will open the doors into answers of the unknown—answers for your personal growth.

Take as much time as needed for communing with your tool, then allow yourself time to clear your mind and relax thoroughly. If you feel anxious, nervous, or as if you cannot physically hold still long enough to complete this exercise, don't worry. You can always try again. Do not overwhelm yourself.

Take a few minutes to rest. In this next phase of the exercise you should share your dreams, questions, and energies with your tool. Explore in your mind all the magical work you and the tool will conduct together. Channel yourself, in energy form, into the tool; feel it channeling its energy to you. Visualize this in any color or form desired. You may envision a stream of vivid blue light creeping up your hand and arm, and being absorbed into your body. Proceed slowly. Allow an exchange of messages, symbols, and imagery to occur between you and the tool. Breathe smoothly and stay relaxed.

The last phase of this exercise should be spent in exploring the depths of your tool's energies. No matter what images come to mind, make a mental note to remember each one. Afterward, you can record the images into a notebook to interpret them later.

When you are ready to conclude the exercise, thank the tool's energies for the time shared. Express your appreciation for its wisdom and insights. Breathe normally. You will feel relaxed, refreshed, and consciously awakened. Open your eyes. Let them adjust to focus and light. Stretch your muscles before standing upright or preparing to move around. If you have a pen and notebook at your side, make a record of your experience. This will guide you back to full waking consciousness.

The previous meditation and bonding exercise was written for solitary practice, however it may also be used as a guided meditation for two or more people. One person can read the meditation aloud, softly and slowly, to the entire group. If you have a cassette recorder, you can narrate the meditation onto a tape to play back to yourself during performance of the exercise. This may be much easier than attempting to read or memorize it.

The next meditation exercise is one that exercises the psyche at a more advanced level than the previous bonding exercise. The basic techniques of relaxation and meditation described in this meditation are similar to those of the preceding exercise. However, this meditation is designed to help you explore the depths of your psyche more vigorously.

If you decide to tape the meditation for your own use, remember to speak gently, clearly, and slowly. A soft, slow voice reciting the meditation will allow your mind to fully produce imagery, react, and absorb wisdom from your higher self.

The Pathway of Trees Meditation

A comfortable, quiet space with as few distractions as possible is necessary for this meditation. This exercise may be conducted as casually or formally as you would like. Your comfort is the main consideration. Don't burn incense or use accessories that alter or distract the attention of your senses. You only need your ritual tool, which should be held lightly upon your lap if you are seated or laid upon your abdomen if you are lying down.

Begin by using the breathing and relaxation practices that were described in the bonding exercise. It is very important that you be relaxed and in a tranquil state of mind.

As soon as you are ready, close your eyes and envision a wooded pathway in front of you. See yourself standing before it and take in the images of the deep green forest foliage and the brown path strewn with stones and pebbles. You hear bird calls and the rustling of tree branches as a cool wind sails along the path. You feel an ultimate sense of serenity and a unity with everything that appears, or does not appear, around you. Your everyday worries and concerns are gone. You have projected yourself, through your mind, away from the chaos of the modern world. All phobias and fears have been left behind in your physical body, which at this time lies resting. Any animals or creatures you see do not frighten you or make you feel anxious. You are extremely calm, as if you know this place, the place which awakens your spiritual senses.

As you look down the pathway, focus on the trees which surround the path on either side. They are majestic and tall, and you find yourself coaxed by their presence to walk down the path. They are the guardians of the path. The trees emit a sense of serenity—the same tranquillity that you feel deep within you.

You begin down the path, gazing up toward the shelter of high tree branches as you travel. Looking in front of you, you can see the path in the distance reaching upward as you approach a small hill. You move up the hill as you follow the path. Notice that you are not out of breath. You travel with ease. At the top of the hill, the path curves and twists through a lush forest. Suddenly, you find yourself overlooking a clearing of vibrant green grass encircled by trees. As you enter the middle of the clearing, you stop and turn to look in all directions. The pathway is gone—vanished. The trees now completely enclose the circular clearing. You are not shocked or fearful at this event, however. The trees are protective; they welcome you with their wisdom.

You move toward the outline of trees encircling the clearing. Your hand reaches out to touch one of the tree trunks; your hand and the tree bark beneath it vibrate with energy. You feel the tree's life force. You are drawn to this particular tree. You desire to know about the energy you feel within it. You sit at the base of the tree, reclining against the bumpy, yet comfortable tree trunk. Feel its massive strength supporting you.

The surrounding area is very tranquil. You feel yourself mesmerized by the vibrational rhythm of energy extending from the tree trunk and absorbed into your being. No words are spoken, yet you realize there is an awareness—a form of communication that exists between you and the tree, and the knowledge shared is immense. You lean your head back against the trunk's bark, and as you do so, images and visions fill your mind. You feel yourself becoming one with the tree. You are going backwards in time, to a moment that is lost in the mists of antiquity. You are going to visit the tree's ancient past—a period in time that has much to teach you.

As you experience deeper relaxation, your breathing becomes more rhythmic and slow. Your mind is crystal clear, and a spectrum of colors engulfs your inner vision. You swim through the colors with ease and come to a vast emptiness, which you swim through as well. As you swim through this emptiness, you slowly become solid and immovable. You sense the existence of other beings, and you dance slowly in circles in their presence. As you dance, you feel the churning of an inner fire, and you sense chaos, which quickly decreases until it subsides completely. Your mind's eye sees huge ridges of the Earth, which are towering mountains reaching as far as the mind's eye can see. You float through their caverns and enter deep valleys. Below, you see winding brooks, valleys, fields, and woodland terrain.

You are passing through time. The inner fires ignite once again as you pass over oceans and shorelines. You thrust upward toward the cloudless, blue sky and the seasons of summer, fall, winter, and spring—birth, growth, death, and rebirth. You become one with the Turning Wheel, the Wheel of Life. Each season batters your being with rain, thunderstorm, sun, wind, snow. Each passing season flows over your being, smoothing and washing away tension.

You feel the thrust of growth within you. Your arms stretch high toward the sky, as you reach for the brilliant rays of the sun. Your feet plant themselves deeper into the cool, life-giving soil of the Earth. You feel your legs stretching farther and farther as your feet and toes extend themselves in their struggle to penetrate the deep core of the Earth's soil.

Clouds gather overhead, and the blackened sky erupts with lightning. Waves of thunder shudder within you. You hear a heavy rain falling. It splatters noisily upon you. You feel the water's coolness and are nourished by the nutrients it brings.

This storm will pass, and time crawls by as you stand implanted in the Earth and stretching into the sky. With each passing moment there are animals and plants who come to find shelter within your outstretched arms and at the base of your rooted feet. One day, sentient animals come. They have studied and worshipped the Sun, Moon, and the Earth. They understand who you are and the wisdom that you hold. Carefully, and with utmost respect, they cut away smaller branches of your magnificent arms to use for their devotional rites. They chant and sing hymns as they work; as they take a portion of you away to a distant place.

A branch that was removed from you is taken to a new place. A portion of your energy is within it. Your presence is in several places at once—like a candle flame that is used to light several candles. The sentient creatures have shaped and carved the branches of your being, and you are held with honor as the rituals of spirit and magic are performed. Pharaohs hold you upon their throne; shamans raise you skyward to the Great Spirit; and medicine men and women wave your branch soothingly over the sick in order to heal them. Viking ships have anchored upon new lands, and the warriors conquer their enemies with your strength in hand.

The sun, moon, and seasons still pass over your branch in precise cycles. You know of their comings and goings, and you commune with each passage.

The sentient creatures known as humans come to honor you and extract your energies and wisdom for powerful rituals, both divine and magical. Like you, they recognize the passage of the sun, moon, and seasons, and honor the Turning Wheel of Life. You share your special awareness of these events with the humans. You desire to fulfill their needs for wisdom, their striving for communion with the secrets you hold. Yet the humans have a limited comprehension of these things. You feel lonely in the knowledge that you have no way to completely unveil these secrets to their understanding.

Then, one day, a human comes to you, takes you into their hands gently, speaks to you, and asks to share the wisdom and knowledge that you hold. Upon this ritualistic bonding, you share the events of your life, the passage of time you've witnessed, and your kinship of all creatures of air and land. This human understands and rejoices in your teachings. The loneliness you once felt now subsides as you share a closeness with this human; revealing knowledge never before revealed: what you've seen, heard, learned, experienced, what you believe, and what you understand.

[**Note:** Pause here for a short period of rhythmic breathing. Meditate upon your ritual tool and what knowledge it may have to share. If you are solitary, then pause for at least a minute or two. If you are narrating for a group, or another person, allow silence for the next couple of minutes—enough time for everyone to absorb the knowledge of their tool—then continue the narration.]

The sun sets, and the human moves away from you, becoming more and more distant. The physical distance is great, yet the spiritual connection is forever close.

You take a deep breath and find yourself awakened, leaning against the trunk of your chosen tree. You awaken to the knowledge that a spiritual connection has been formed between you and the ritual tool you hold. You arise from your meditation at the base of the great tree. You turn and face the tree. You understand each other. You now have an understanding of the gift that you hold—your ritual tool. This gift is a symbol of the heritage, the passage of time, the passage of the Wheel of Life, and of the knowledge that the tree has shared. It has given a part of itself, its wisdom, to be with you always.

You stand and thank the tree for its teachings. You turn, ritual tool in hand, and walk down the pathway once again visible through the circle of trees. You understand the wisdom and messages that the pathway of trees has granted you. You share in their extended strength and security.

Treading once more upon the path, you pass all manner of creatures without fear. You carefully descend down the hill, and walk, feeling refreshed and renewed, back to the beginning of the path. Once there, you turn, facing the pathway as you first did, and sit down. You feel relaxed, and you allow yourself to re-awaken into your physical body. Return to normal waking consciousness. Rest for a few moments. Hold your ritual tool gently and commune with it. Feel the bond that now exists. Quietly rejoice in feeling the bond with the ancient spirit of the tree—the bond you've developed with your ritual tool.

This meditation is what many consider a "guided visualization," which often is narrated by one individual and experienced by another or an entire group. This meditation would be quite effective for a group because it consists entirely of mental imagery—there is no physical movement involved that might cause distractions in a large group.

It is interesting to note that many pagan and shamanic religions use some kind of meditation to acquaint the practitioner with a new ritual tool. Wicca has dedication and consecration rituals, both consisting of a meditation designed to create a bond between the witch and tool. All pagan religions and magical systems have similar instructions for such a process. A consecration ceremony reminds the practitioner that a ritual tool is not an ordinary utensil, but rather a special item that contains spiritual energies.

Consecration of Your Ritual Tools

Consecration of your ritual tools is not merely performed in order to clean each article of negative energies that may be present, but also to charge it with your own energies or demonstrate reverence toward the tree spirit from which the wood came. Consecration is a primary step in reinforcing the bond between you and your ritual tool and preparing it for ritual use.

No one knows the exact moment in history when humans began consecrating ritual tools and objects. Every religion practices consecration in one fashion or another. In Christianity, the priest serving the bread and wine, which represents Jesus Christ's body and blood, blesses and consecrates these two sacred items before administering them to followers. In the Wiccan religion, consecration rites are used to sanctify ritual tools, cakes and ale, and a variety of other items and events.

Before using your ritual tools, it is necessary to cleanse them and dedicate each one to the work you will conduct with them. There are numerous ways to accomplish this task, depending upon your particular spiritual path. The following consecration ritual is Wiccan in content and flavor. Feel free, however, to change it to better suit your personal spiritual practice, or develop your own ritual for this purpose.

Consecration Ritual

For the purpose of presenting this ceremony, we will describe the consecration of a ritual knife, although the name of any other ritual tool can be substituted for the word "knife" in this text.

Preparation

Your sacred space, a private area of your home, or a peaceful spot outdoors are all ideal locations for the performance of the consecration ritual. You may conduct this rite as formally or informally as you would like. We suggest taking a ceremonial approach, since consecration is an important ritual and worthy of pageantry.

Incense

Incense is a time-honored staple in several religious and magical functions. Many people are familiar with the swinging metal censer used by the Catholic church. You may wish to use a censer, or container for holding incense, in your consecration ritual. Your censer may be as elaborate as that seen in church, or it may be as simple and natural as a sea shell. Whatever you use must be fire proof and able to resist the heat of burning incense. A bowl or cup half filled with salt can be used as a censer; the salt will absorb the heat and prevent the bowl from cracking.

Incense provides a pleasant aroma and aids in changing consciousness during ritual. Some pagans and ceremonial magicians command spirits, deities, or other beings to appear in the rising incense smoke. At times the swirling smoke yields curious shapes, and your deity may be visible within it. Slowly breathing in the aroma of the incense is relaxing and entrancing; you find yourself slipping easily into an alternate plane of consciousness. Incense is used to purify sacred space and is sometimes used to represent the element of air.

Salt and Water

Salt and water are used for the purification of sacred space and consecration of ritual tools. The Holy Water used by some Christian sects serves a similar purpose. In paganism it is thought that sprinkling saltwater throughout a home, sacred space, or on ritual tools, releases energies within the salt to be directed and magnified by the practitioner's will or intent. This technique, combined with visualization can be used to rid oneself of any negative or disturbing energies.

Place a pinch of salt into a cup, put some water into another cup. The salt and water will be mixed during the ritual at the appropriate time.

Attire

Take a cleansing ritual bath beforehand. Then, dress comfortably in a long, flowing robe without shoes, jewelry, or additional clothing. A robe is traditional in many pagan religions and magical groups, though several witchcraft traditions prefer to work naked (skyclad) to symbolize the pure and simple way that our physical bodies came into this world. This is fine if temperature and privacy permit. Both ways of presenting yourself to your deities, robed or skyclad, are intended to create a separation between the practitioner and the mundane world.

If you have an altar, place your ritual tool, incense, and salt and water upon it. If you do not have an altar, any table or surface will do.

Once prepared, light four candles to represent the four elements— Air, Earth, Fire, and Water—at the four corners of your room or ritual circle. Turn off the lights.

The Ceremony

Smell the exotic aroma of the incense. Watch the dancing flames of the candles, and allow yourself to depart from the mundane world around you. Invoke your deities to join in your ritual and witness the consecration.

Take up your ritual tool and hold it high into the air in salute and call upon your deities.

> (State the names of your God, Goddess, or divine source here), *My Lord and Lady; the Father of all life and Mother of all creatures that live;*
>
> *From the materials of nature I have fashioned this ritual tool into the form before you.*
>
> *I present this ritual knife for your approval, since it shall function in thy service.*

Place the ritual tool on your altar or table top. Relax for a moment of meditation, remembering the time, effort, and creativity you put into fashioning this tool—a tool that is truly your own. When ready, pour the salt into the cup holding the water and mix thoroughly with your index finger. Dip your fingers into the saltwater mixture and sprinkling it over your ritual tool; first one side of the tool and then the other. Next, pass the ritual tool through the rising smoke of the burning incense while saying:

I exorcise thee, O knife of steel, with this creature of salt and water, and the smoke of holy incense.

I cast out from thee all impurities and uncleanness in the names of the Father God and Mother Goddess. (You may insert the names of your deities).

Hold the ritual tool firmly in both hands. Using visualization and focusing all of your energies, concentrate upon charging the ritual tool with your power, then say:

I charge this ritual knife by the wisdom and powers of the omnipresent God and Goddess; By the virtue of the universe and the power of the elements, I shall obtain whatever service that I desire from you. So mote it be.

The consecration is complete. You may wish to continue the ritual and consecrate other ritual tools, jewelry, and additional items. Or you may stay spend more time venerating your deity. When you are ready to close the ritual, gives thanks to those divine beings you invoked to witness and assist in the consecration. You may close the ceremony in whatever manner your spiritual tradition prescribes.

After the tool has been consecrated, some religions dictate that the tool is to be carried by the practitioner constantly for twenty-four hours, placed in moonlight overnight, or placed on a pentagram until its first use in ritual. Other religions strictly advise that the consecrated tool be put to use immediately. In our own spiritual practice, we either wrap the consecrated tool in a white linen handkerchief and place it in a storage box upon our altar, or lay it upon the altar over a pentagram or another protective, charging symbol. What you do with your newly consecrated tool is entirely your decision.

If you craft a ritual tool for another individual, you may wish to consecrate it before introducing the tool to its new owner. This is often performed merely out of good will, especially if the individual plans on using the tool immediately upon receiving it. Ask the person if they would like you to consecrate their tool for them.

Some pagan religions also perform a dedication ritual immediately after the consecration ritual. This dedication is intended to validate and honor the new implement as a functioning tool for the service of one's deities, although we personally feel that the consecration ritual already accomplished this.

Each ritual tool you create and use is a sacred implement; it is personal and unique. Your tool should not be lent to others, or carelessly thrown in a closet. Ritual tools are for spiritual and magical workings. They are also to be proudly displayed. You have worked diligently to craft your tool and have adorned it with the beauty of your personal symbolism. Why keep it hidden from others? Our ritual tools are displayed upon an antique table in our library. We enjoy viewing their artistic beauty often, and we enjoy sharing the energies of our tools with all who view them.

May your self-created ritual tools serve you well, and may you continue to use your creativity in all areas of your life. Never refuse to try or to learn something new just because you doubt your ability to succeed. Attempt the feat before admitting defeat. The challenge may present failure at first, but keep trying. You will succeed.

We hope that the information contained in this book will stimulate new areas of learning and discovery in your life. Allow yourself to be open to new ideas, concepts, and knowledge. May the Gods and Goddesses guide you and bless you. Blessed Be!

Resources Guide

The following catalog retailers may carry supplies you will find help-ful in constructing your ritual tools, specifically the Sword Staff and the Ritual Knife.

The Noble Collection
P.O. Box 1476
Sterling, VA 21067
1-800-8NOBLE8
(1-800-866-2538)
A source for swords, daggers, and knives.

Crazy Crow Trading Post
1801 North Airport Road
Pottsboro, TX 75076
903-786-2287
A source for a wide variety of knife blades and knives.

Suggested Reading

Celtic Tree Magic

Glass-Koentop, Pattalee. *Year of the Moon, Season of Trees; Mysteries & Rites of Celtic Tree Magic*. St. Paul: Llewellyn Publications, 1990.

Hope, Murry. *Practical Celtic Magic*. London: The Aquarian Press, 1987.

Magic

Cunningham, Scott and David Harrington. *Spell Crafts: Crafting Magical Objects*. St. Paul: Llewellyn Publications, 1993.

Gonzalez-Wippler, Migene. *The Complete Book of Spells, Ceremonies & Magic*. St. Paul: Llewellyn Publications, 1978.

Gundarsson, Kveldulf. *Teutonic Magic: The Magical & Spiritual Practices of the Germanic Peoples*. St. Paul: Llewellyn Publications, 1990.

Kraig, Donald Michael. *Modern Magick: Eleven Lessons in the High Magickal Arts*. St. Paul: Llewellyn Publications, 1988.

Lady Sabrina, *Reclaiming the Power: The How and Why of Practical Ritual Magic*. St. Paul: Llewellyn Publications, 1992.

Reed, Ellen Cannon. *Invocation of the Gods: Ancient Egyptian Magic for Today*. St. Paul: Llewellyn Publications, 1992.

Regardie, Israel. *The Golden Dawn: The Original Account of the Teachings, Rites & Ceremonies of the Hermetic Order*. St. Paul: Llewellyn Publications, 1989.

Runes

Peschel, Lisa. *A Practical Guide to the Runes: Their Use in Divination and Magick*. St. Paul: Llewellyn Publications, 1989.

Thorrson, Edred. *Rune-Might: Secret Practices of the German Rune Magicians*. St. Paul: Llewellyn Publications, 1989.

Thorrson, Edred. *The Nine Doors of Midgard: A Complete Curriculum of Rune Magic*. St. Paul: Llewellyn Publications, 1991.

Willis, Tony. *The Runic Workbook: Understanding and Using the Power of Runes*. New York: Sterling Publishing, 1990.

Shamanism: Including Texts of Tools and Their Use

Meadows, Kenneth. *Shamanic Experience: A Practical Guide to Contemporary Shamanism*. Rockford, MA: Element Inc., 1991.

Sun Bear, Wabun Wind, and Crysalis Mulligan, *Dancing with the Wheel: The Medicine Wheel Workbook*. New York: Simon & Schuster, 1991.

Wolfe, Amber. *In the Shadow of the Shaman: Connecting with Self, Nature and Spirit*. St. Paul: Llewellyn Publications, 1988.

Symbols, Sigils and Alphabets

Frater U.D., *Practice Sigil Magic: Creating Personal Symbols for Success*. St. Paul: Llewellyn Publications, 1990.

Hulse, David Allen. *The Key of It All, Book One: The Eastern Mysteries*. St. Paul: Llewellyn Publications, 1996.
Secret symbolism and true alphabet magic of every ancient Eastern magical tradition.

Thorrson, Edred. *The Book of Ogham: The Celtic Tree Oracle*. St. Paul: Llewellyn Publications, 1992.

Whitcomb, Bill. *The Magician's Companion: A Practical and Encyclopedic Guide to Magical and Religious Symbolism*. St. Paul: Llewellyn Publications, 1993.

Also see Buckland, Raymond under "Wicca".

Wicca: Including Texts of Tools and Their Use

Alder, Margot. *Drawing Down The Moon*. Boston: Beacon Press, 1981.

Buckland, Raymond. *Buckland's Complete Book of Witchcraft*. St. Paul: Llewellyn Publications, 1990.

Campanelli, Pauline. *Wheel of the Year: Living The Magical Life*. St. Paul: Llewellyn Publications, 1992.

Cunningham, Scott. *Wicca: A Guide for the Solitary Practitioner*. St. Paul: Llewellyn Publications, 1990.

Farrar, Janet, and Stewart Farrar. *A Witches Bible Compleat*. New York City: Magickal Childe Publishing Inc., 1981, 1984.

Stein, Diane. *Casting the Circle: A Women's Book of Ritual*, Freedom,CA: The Crossing Press, 1990.

Wood Carving

Skinner, Freda. *Wood Carving*. New York: Bonanza Books, MCMLXI.

Wood Working

Bass, Gene and Jack Portice. *Carving Weathered Wood*.
This book includes award winning woodcarvings. The text discusses the first step of planning a project to its completion. Teaches how to also carve gorgeous statues and figures.

Frank, George. *Wood Finishing with George Frank*.
Tips from a renowned expert in woodworking. 80 full color photos and wonderful text of unique and stunning finishes you can accomplish on different wood.

Hoadley, R. Bruce. *Understanding Wood: A Craftsman's Guide to Wood Technology.*

Korn, Peter. *Working With Wood: The Basics of Craftsmanship.*
A step-by-step introduction to traditional woodworking. The text concentrates on using hand tools instead of power tools. A perfect guide for beginners.

Naylor, Maria editor. *Authentic Indian Designs.*
Contains 2,500 illustrations of Indian designs for carving, painting and a variety of uses.

Tangerman, E.J. *Complete Guide to Woodcarving.*

Tangerman, E.J. *Whittling and Woodcarving.*
An excellent source for learning whittling and woodcarving techniques. Mr. Tangerman's motto is, "if you can cut a potato you can carve."

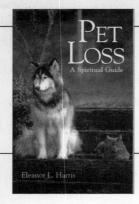

Pet Loss
A Spiritual Guide

Eleanor L. Harris

The grief that follows the death of a pet has only recently been recognized and treated by the mental health community. While it is absolutely normal and healthy to mourn, the grieving process can be crippling emotionally, mentally, and even physically. Here is the first book to examine how to cope with this unique loss from a broad, spiritual perspective. It addresses the emotional responses of the grieving process, the pros and cons of euthanasia, and the logistics of making final arrangements for your pet's body. You will learn the psychological facts about the human-animal bond; how to deal with the initial shock of your loss, as well as your anger, guilt, and sadness; and the truth about what happens at the cemetery or crematorium. Various religious beliefs are presented, with a focus on pagan funeral rituals and meditations.

1-56718-347-6, 288 pgs., ⅜₆ x 8, illus., softbound $9.95

Mad About Mead
Nectar of the Gods

Pamela Spence

Mead—it was the elixir of red-bearded Vikings and sloe-eyed Sheba. Ancient peoples believed that drinking the fermented honey imparted the divine gifts of prophecy, poetry and fertility. Far from being an historical oddity, however, mead is now enjoying an international revival.

Mad About Mead is geared to those who are intrigued by the "idea" of mead as well as to those who actually make it. Written in a light-hearted, humorous style, it is an eclectic mix of history, mythology, rituals and instructions. The detailed recipe section has information about honey varieties, yeasts, equipment, and problem solving, plus a chapter on commercial mead production. You will find directions for brewing pumpkin mead (right in the pumpkin) alongside lab-tested recipes for melomel ... and recipes using bee pollen and forage fruit alongside recipes using commercial yeast energizers and acid blends. The resource section will point you to others who share the mead madness.

1-56718-683-1, 6 x 9, 208 pp., illus., softcover $12.95

To order, call 1–800–THE MOON
Prices subject to change without notice